# Better French
## Achieving fluency with everyday speech

# Studymates

British History 1870–1918: The Emergence of a Nation
War: How War Became Global
Hitler and Nazi Germany: The Seduction of a Nation (3rd ed)
The English reformation: The Effect on a Nation
European History 1870–1918: The Rise of Nationalism
Lenin, Stalin and Communist Russia: The Myth and Reality of
    Communism
Genetics: The Science of Genetics Revealed (2nd ed)
Organic Chemistry: How Organic Chemistry Works (2nd ed)
Chemistry: A's Chemistry Explained
Chemistry: Chemistry Calculations Explained
The New Science Teacher's Handbook
Mathematics for Adults: Basic Mathematics Explained
Calculus: How Calculus Works
Understanding Forces: How Forces Work
Algebra: Basic Algebra Explained
Plant Physiology: The Structure of Plants Explained
Poems to Live By
Shakespeare: The Barriers Removed
Chaucer: Approaching the Canterbury Tales
Poetry: The Secret Gems of Poetry Revealed
Better English: Handle Everyday Situations with Confidence
Better French: Become Fluent with Everyday Speech
Social Anthropology: Investigating Human Social Life
Statistics for Social Science: Data Handling Explained
Study Skills: Maximise Your Time to Pass Exams
Practical Drama and Theatre Arts: Practical Theatre Skills
    Explained
The War Poets 1914–18: The Secrets of Poems from the Great
    War
The Academic Essay: How to Plan, Draft, Write and Revise
Your Masters Thesis: How to Plan, Draft, Write and Revise
Your PhD Thesis: How to Plan, Draft, Write, Revise and Edit
    Your Thesis

*Many other titles in preparation*

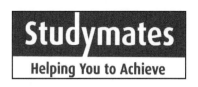

# Better French

## Achieving fluency with everyday speech

*3rd edition*

**Monique Jackman**

www.studymates.co.uk

**ISBN-10** 1-84285-066-0
**ISBN-13** 978-1-84285-066-4

First published 2000
Reprinted 2001 (Twice)
Second edition 2004
Third edition 2005

This edition published by Studymates Limited, Studymates
House, Abergele, Conwy-County LL22 8DD,
United Kingdom.

Typeset by PDQ Typesetting, Newcastle-under-Lyme
Printed and Bound in the United Kingdom by the Bell &
Bain Ltd, Glasgow

# Contents

# Preface

After five years of learning French at school – or about three in adult education, and especially when studying French for A level and at university – adults and teenagers who want to become fluent in French seem to stumble on certain everyday words, phrases and expressions. In the case of certain words, they also stumble on the different pronunciations that they can have.

For example, what's the difference between *se promener* and *marcher*? Which should you use: *connaître* or *savoir*, *partir* or *quitter*, *en avance* or *tôt*? Are *donc* and *alors* interchangeable? What about *grand* and *gros*? Is there a difference between *conduire* and *rouler*? Why can't *prendre* translate *to take* someone somewhere? When do you use *c'est* and *il est*? Can you explain *s'agir*? What is the French for *to enjoy*? There are several ways to say *don't mention it*. Which is the best one? When do you pronounce the final 's' in *plus*?

These are a few of the common questions which always seem to cause students trouble and worry when a certain level is reached. Dictionaries seem to be either too big and detailed, or too small with just basic or general definitions: what is needed is a class-room explanation, and lots of examples to illustrate differences.

This Studymate is a book of classroom explanations for such questions. It is something between a textbook and a dictionary, an effective short cut to fluency in French. It also shows that the difficulties encountered are *not* endless, as many students fear. You will soon see how 'full pictures' emerge.

With this book, you will quickly learn the right way to use 'problem words'. In the examples, both vocabulary and grammar have been deliberately kept simple, so you can concentrate on spotting the differences between sets of words, and study concise explanations until your understanding is complete. Fluency is within your grasp!

*Monique Jackman*

*mjackman@studymates.co.uk*

# Choosing the Correct Verb

Choosing the correct verb is a big step towards fluency. For example, *to leave* is *partir* when it can be translated with *to leave* as in to go. It is *quitter* when *leaving* someone or something, and it is *laisser* when *leaving* someone or something somewhere. *Prendre* is *to take* but is not much use for translating *to take* things or people from A to B. For example, *emmener* is the right verb when taking someone somewhere, *emporter* or *prendre* when taking something with you, *porter* when you take, as in carry, something somewhere, or to someone, and *conduire* when taking somebody, as in show somebody the way. A number of other verbs need careful explanations. This chapter will show you:

- the correct verb for *to walk*
- the correct verb for *to start*
- the correct verb for *to drive*
- the correct verb for *to know*
- the correct verb for *to decide to*
- the correct verb for *to take*
- the correct verb for *to cook*
- the correct verb for *to look after*
- the correct verb for *to enjoy*
- the correct verb for *to leave*
- the correct verb for *to think*
- the correct verb for *to take time*

# Aller/rentrer/venir à pied, marcher, se promener/faire une promenade, faire de la marche – *to walk*

## Aller/rentrer/venir à pied

Le lundi, je *vais* à l'école *à pied*. On Mondays, I *walk* to school.

Je *suis venu à pied* aujourd'hui. I *walked* (here) today.

Demain j'*irai* à la bibliothèque *à pied*. I'll *walk* to the library tomorrow.

Vous pourriez *venir à pied*, ce n'est pas loin. You could *walk* (here) it's not far.

Est-ce qu'elle *va* au travail *à pied*. Does she *walk* to work?

Je *suis rentré à pied* parce que je n'avais pas d'argent pour le bus. I *walked* home because I didn't have any money for the bus.

- Use *aller à pied, rentrer à pied* or *venir à pied* to say two things in one go: to go somewhere, and how (means of transport), in this case, *walking*.

## Marcher

Il a commencé à *marcher* à un an. He started *to walk* when he was one.

Il faut *marcher* plus vite. You must *walk* faster.

On *a marché* pendant vingt minutes avant de trouver l'hôtel. We *walked* for twenty minutes before finding the hotel.

Pourquoi *marchez*-vous si lentement? Why *are* you *walking* so slowly?

Après son accident, il lui a fallu réapprendre à *marcher*. After his/her accident, he/she had to learn (how) *to walk* again.

J'ai si mal aux jambes aujourd'hui que je ne peux pas *marcher*. My legs ache so much today, that I cannot *walk*.

● *Marcher* is used to talk about the action of walking.

## Se promener/faire une promenade

J'aime *me promener* tous les dimanches. I like *going for a walk* every Sunday.

S'il ne pleuvait pas nous pourrions *faire une promenade* dans le bois. If it wasn't raining, we could *go for a walk* in the woods.

Ils *se sont promenés* toute la matinée. They walked (*went for a walk* for) the whole morning.

Où peut-on *se promener*, près d'ici? Where can one *go for a walk* near here?

Nous *nous promènerons* ensemble. *We'll go for a walk* together.

On *fait une promenade*? Shall we *go for a walk*?

● *Se promener* and *faire une promenade* are interchangeable. They both mean *to go for a walk* or *to go for a stroll*. They both imply walking leisurely, possibly as an occasional pastime.

## Faire de la marche

Nous *faisons de la marche* tous les week-ends. We *walk*/go walking every weekend.

*Faire de la marche* est excellent pour la santé. *Walking* is excellent for health.

J'aimerais *faire de la marche*, mais je n'ai jamais le temps. I'd love *to go walking*/take up walking, but I never have the time.

En vacances, je *fais* beaucoup *de marche*. I *walk*/do a lot of walking when I am on holiday.

Depuis quand *faites*-vous de la *marche*? How long *have* you *been walking* for (as a hobby)?

Vous n'avez pas besoin d'argent pour *faire de la marche*. You don't need money *to go walking*/to take up walking.

● *Faire de la marche* means to walk, *to go walking* as a sport, implying a regular hobby.

### Also useful to know

1. The noun, **une promenade** is 'a walk'. To 'walk the dog' is **promener** (not reflexive) le chien. When asking for directions, instead of saying 'vous continuez jusqu'aux feux' (you carry on until you reach the traffic lights) it is possible that a French person might say: vous **marchez** jusqu'aux feux (whether you're on foot or in a car!)

2. If mechanical things (camera, television, washing machine or even the car) do not 'work', the verb you need is **marcher**: 'La télévision ne marche pas.' (The television does not work.)

3. **Ça marche**?, or, comment ça marche? are familiar ways of saying ça va?/Comment ça va?/Comment allez-vous? (how is it going?). Similarly **tout marche bien** means 'all is well/all is going well.'

4. **Faire marcher quelqu'un**, means, 'to pull someone's leg': 'Est-ce que vous me faites marcher?' (Are you pulling my leg?)

# Commencer, se mettre à – *to start*

## Commencer/commencer à

Il n'*a* pas encore *commencé*. He *has*n't *started* yet.

On *a commencé à* écrire les cartes postales. We'*ve started* writing the postcards.

Elles ne peuvent pas commencer avant mardi. They can't *start* before Tuesday.

Quand *a*-t-elle *commencé à* marcher? When *did* she start to walk?

Je *commencerai à* lire le livre ce soir. I'*ll start* reading the book tonight.

Ma soeur a décidé de *commencer* son ménage de printemps ce week-end. My sister has decided *to start* her spring cleaning this weekend.

On ne *commence à* vendre des glaces qu'à partir de juin là-bas. They only *start* selling ice creams from June over there.

Quel jour *commencerez*-vous? What/which day *will* you *start*?

Ils *ont commencé* le puzzle. They *have started* the puzzle.

- *To start* something, or to start doing something is *commencer.*

# Se mettre à

Le four *s'est mis à* fumer. The oven *started* to smoke.

Je ne sais pas pourquoi elle *s'est mise à* rougir. I don't know why she *started* blushing.

Michel *s'est mis à* crier sans raison. Michel *started* to scream for no reason.

Dès qu'il les a vus, ils *se sont mis à* courir. As soon as he saw them, they *started* running.

Ce n'est pas la peine de *te mettre à* pleurer. It's no use you *starting* to cry.

Tout à coup elle *s'est mise à* chanter à tue-tête. She suddenly *started* to sing at the top of her voice.

Il faut que tu *te mettes à* étudier. You must *start* studying.

Je *me mettrai au* travail après mon émission préférée. I*'ll start* work after (I've watched) my favourite programme.

Quand Stéphanie a eu treize ans, elle *s'est mise à* faire du patinage. When Stephanie turned thirteen, she *started* going ice-skating.

- *Se mettre à* + infinitive can mean *to start*, and could be replaced with *commencer à*. The slight difference is that *se mettre à* often implies that an action was started as a consequence of something else, or unexpectedly.

# Also useful to know

1. **Se mettre à** can also mean 'to set about' doing something, or 'to get on with' something. It can also be used to translate 'to take up' something.

2. The phrases **s'y mettre** or **y mettre du sien** mean 'to make a good effort', 'to pull one's weight.'

# Conduire, aller/venir en voiture, rouler, prendre la voiture – *to drive*

## Conduire

Votre fils *conduit* depuis combien de temps? How long *has* your son *been driving* for?

Je ne saurai jamais *conduire.* I shall never be able *to drive.*

Mon mari n'aime pas *conduire* la nuit. My husband doesn't like *driving* at night.

Mais tu *conduis* beaucoup trop vite, enfin! You *drive* much too fast!

On *a conduit* pendant trois heures sans s'arrêter. We *drove* for three hours without stopping.

Je déteste *conduire* sur l'autoroute. I hate *driving* on the motorway.

Qui *conduira* demain? Who *is going to drive* tomorrow?

Quand je l'ai vue, elle *conduisait* vers le port. She *was driving* towards the harbour when I saw her.

- With *conduire* the emphasis is on the actual skill, or the actual activity.

## Conduire ( + someone somewhere)

Le voisin l'*a* tout de suite *conduit* à l'hôpital. The neighbour immediately *drove* him to the hospital.

Mon beau-frère pourra nous *conduire* sur la côte pour nos vacances en juin. My brother-in-law will be able *to drive* us to the coast for our holiday in June.

Qui les *conduit* à l'école tous les jours? Who *drives* them to school every day?

Elle voudrait que je la *conduise.* She'd like me *to drive* her.

Il faudrait que quelqu'un me *conduise.* I would need someone *to drive* me.

Mes amis nous *conduiront.* My friends *will drive* us.

* *Conduire* can also be used to translate *to drive someone*/to give someone a lift (as in English, location of course, can be only implied).

## Aller/venir en voiture, prendre la voiture

Je n'aime pas *aller* au travail *en voiture*
> = Je n'aime pas *venir* au travail *en voiture*
> = je n'aime pas *prendre la voiture* pour aller/venir au travail (je prends le car).

I don't like *driving* to work (I come by coach).

Finalement, nous avons décidé d'*aller* à Grenoble *en voiture*
> = Finalement, nous avons décidé de *venir* à Grenoble *en voiture*
> = finalement nous avons décidé de *prendre la voiture* pour aller/venir à Grenoble.

In the end we decided *to drive* to Grenoble.

Est-ce que Martin y *est allé en voiture?*
> = Est-ce que Martin *est venu en voiture?*
> = Est-ce que Martin *a pris la voiture?*

*Did* Martin *drive* (there/here)?

Mes parents ne *vont* jamais au centre-ville *en voiture*
> = Mes parents ne *viennent* jamais au centre-ville *en voiture*
> = Mes parents ne *prennent* jamais *la voiture* pour aller/venir au centre-ville.

My parents never *drive* to the town-centre.

Elle *ira* chez ses amis en Normandie *en voiture*
> = Elle *viendra* chez ses amis en Normandie *en voiture*
> = Elle *prendra la voiture* pour aller/venir chez ses amis.

She *will drive* to her friends' place in Normandy.

Y *êtes*-vous *allé en voiture?*
> = *Êtes*-vous *venu en voiture?*
> = *Avez*-vous *pris la voiture* pour y aller/pour venir?
> *Did* you *drive* (there/here)?

Il vaudra mieux y *aller en voiture*
> = Il vaudra mieux *venir en voiture*
> = Il vaudra mieux *prendre la voiture.*
> It will be better *to drive.*

- When the emphasis is on the means of transport *conduire* can be used, but a native would probably use *aller/venir en voiture* or *prendre la voiture.*

## Rouler

Vous ne savez pas qu'il faut *rouler* à droite ici! Don't you know that you have *to drive* on the right here!

Après avoir *roulé* pendant deux heures, nous nous sommes arrêtés dans un joli petit village. After *driving* for two hours, we stopped in a lovely little village.

Tu peux *rouler* un peu moins vite, j'ai peur moi. Can you *drive* a bit slower, I'm scared.

Je *roulais* tranquillement sur le Grand Boulevard quand la voiture devant moi s'est mise à klaxonner bruyamment. I *was driving* on the Grand Boulevard, minding my own business, when the car in front of me suddenly started to blow its horn like mad.

On *roulera* toute la nuit. We'*ll drive* the whole night.

Je viens de la voir *rouler* vers la cathédrale. I've just seen her *driving* towards the cathedral.

Ils n'ont pu *rouler* que très très lentement à cause du brouillard. They could only *drive* very very slowly because of the fog.

- *Rouler* is a bit complicated. *Rouler* is an alternative to *conduire* only when the emphasis is on the actual activity (in other words to say what you are doing, or how) and can also be used to say where you are, but not where you are going!

## Also useful to know

1. It is also helpful to explain when **rouler** can never be used:

    – To talk about the actual skill (Je vais apprendre à conduire l'année prochaine. I'm going to learn to drive next year).

    – When the destination is mentioned, note that 'towards', however, counts as 'where you are' as opposed to the destination (On est allé à Lyon en voiture parce que les trains étaient en grève. We drove to Lyon because the trains were on strike).

    – To talk about the means of transport (j'irai au collège en voiture demain. I'll drive to college tomorrow).

2. **Se promener/faire une promenade/faire un tour en voiture**
   These all mean 'to go for a (car) ride'.

# Connaître, savoir – *to know*

## Connaître + people, or connaître + a place

Est-ce que vous *connaissez* Sylvie. Do you *know* Sylvie?

Ils ne nous *connaissent* pas. They don't *know* us.

Nous *connaissons* son fils depuis trois ans. We'*ve known* his/ her son for three years.

Elle *connaît* bien l'Allemagne. She *knows* Germany very well.

Je regrette, je ne *connais* pas le Restaurant de l'Ile. I'm sorry I do not *know* the Restaurant de l'Ile.

Elles *connaissent* tous mes cousins. They *know* all my cousins.

- *Connaître* is the correct verb to say you *know* people or places.

## Connaître + other nouns

Vous *connaissez* bien la Bouillabaisse? You do *know* what
   Bouillabaisse is, don't you?

Je ne *connais* pas cette chanson. I don't *know* this song.

Mon amie *connaît* mes goûts. My friend *knows* my taste.

Nous *avons connu* le désespoir. We *have known*
   (experienced) despair.

Comment! Il ne *connaît* pas la pétanque! What! He doesn't
   *know* what pétanque is!

Il n'*avait* jamais *connu* tant de succès. He *had* never *known*
   so much success.

Nous *connaissons* un bon bar près d'ici. We *know* a good
   bar near here.

• *Connaître* is also the right choice to translate *to know* + any
   other nouns.

## Savoir

Nous ne *savons* pas de quel quai le train pour Lille part. We
   don't *know* which platform the train to Lille is leaving
   from.

*Savez*-vous combien de jours il restera chez vous? Do you
   *know* how many days he will stay at your house?

Il ne *sait* pas où il a laissé ses lunettes. He doesn't *know*
   where he has left his glasses.

Je *sais* qu'il est retraité. I *know* that he is retired.

On ne *sait* pas quand ils partiront. We don't *know* when
   they will leave.

Je ne *sais* pas ce que je vais faire. I don't *know* what I am
   going to do.

Ils *savent* que je suis mariée. They *know* that I am married.

Elle ne *savait* pas que je n'aime pas la cuisine chinoise. She
   didn't *know* that I don't like Chinese cooking.

• For *to know* a fact, a piece of information, *savoir* is used.

## Connaître + savoir

Je connais son âge = Je sais quel âge il/elle a.

I know how old he/she is.

Elle ne connaît pas son adresse = Elle ne sait pas où il/elle
habite.
She doesn't know her address/where he/she lives.

On connaît le cassoulet = On sait ce que c'est le cassoulet.
We know what cassoulet is.

Je connais Jacques = Je sais qui est Jacques.
I know Jacques (I know who Jacques is).

- It is possible to use either *connaître* or *savoir* to say the
same thing, slightly differently.

## Connaître + noun = savoir + (what is) noun

Je connais les règles du jeu. = Je sais (quelles sont) les règles
du jeu. I know the rules of the game.

Il connaît son adresse. = Il sait (quelle est) son adresse.
He knows his/her address.

Je connais votre numéro de téléphone. = Je sais (quel est )
votre numéro de téléphone. I know your telephone
number.

Connaissez-vous la date de naissance du bébé de Diane? =
Savez-vous (quelle est) la date de naissance du bébé de
Diane?
Do you know the date of birth of Diane's baby?

- It is also possible to leave out 'what is/are' in sentences
with *savoir*. In this instance the shortened sentence will be
the same as for *connaître*.

## Also useful to know

1. 'Je ne **sais** pas' (where the station is – at what time the
film starts – who she is – when the plane goes – if they
like snails, etc) is the French sentence all students
quickly learn, to say 'I do not **know**'. French people

also use three other sentences which could be surprising in view of their literal translations: **Je suis incapable de vous le dire** 'I couldn't tell you' (because I don't know), **je l'ignore** 'I don't know' (although, **ignorer** can also mean 'to ignore') and **c'est pas évident** 'I don't know/you never know'. Examples:

- A quelle heure le magasin ouvre? Ah, ça, je suis incapable de vous le dire. What time does the shop open? (I am afraid) I couldn't tell you (because I don't know).
- Qu'est-ce qu'ils ont répondu? Je l'ignore! I don't know what they replied.
- Oh pardon Monsieur, c'est votre place? C'était pas évident. I'm sorry, is that your seat sir? I didn't know.

2. **Savoir + a verb**

Savoir + a verb, on the other hand, is used to say that you can or can't do a skill. For example:

- Elle sait parler italien. She can (knows how to) speak Italian.
- Sa fille savait lire à trois ans. His/her daughter could (knew how to) read when she was three.
- Savez-vous nager? Can you (do you know how to) swim?
- Qu'est-ce qu'ils savent faire? What can they do?
- J'aimerais savoir conduire. I wish I could drive.

# Décider (de), se décider (à) – to decide (to)

## Décider, décider de

Qui *a décidé de* partir le huit? Who *decided* to leave on the eighth?

Ma soeur *a décidé d'*aller en Espagne cette année. My sister *has decided* to go to Spain this year.

J'*ai décidé de* prendre ma retraite. I*'ve decided* to retire.

Ils *ont décidé de* vendre leur maison et de s'installer sur la
   côte. They've *decided* to sell their house and move to
   the coast.

Elle n'*a* rien *décidé*. She *hasn't decided* anything.

Qu'est-ce que ses beaux-parents *ont décidé*? What *did* his/her
   in-laws *decide*?

Céline vient de *décider* d'acheter un vélo avec l'argent qu'elle
   a gagné. Céline *has* just *decided* to buy a bike with the
   money she has won/earned.

Comment! Vous *aviez décidé* d'y retourner! What! You *had
   decided* to go back there!

Il *avait* déjà *décidé de* lui écrire. He *had* already *decided* to
   write to him/her.

Elle a dit qu'elle *décidera* demain. She said that she *will
   decide* tomorrow.


- Usage of *décider (de)* is straightforward.

## Se décider, se décider à

Vers neuf heures, je *me suis décidé à* téléphoner à Pierre. At
   about nine, *I decided*/I made up my mind/I took the
   decision to phone Pierre.

Quand *s'est*-elle *décidée à* leur parler? When *did* she *decide*/
   make up her mind/take the decision to speak to them?

Il faut *vous décider* tout de suite. You must *decide*/make up
   your mind/take a decision straight away.

Elles ne peuvent pas *se décider*. They cannot *decide*/make up
   their minds/take a decision.

Son frère *s'est décidé à* apprendre à conduire à trente ans.
   His/her brother *decided*/made up his mind/took the
   decision to learn to drive when he was thirty years old.

Nous *nous déciderons* mercredi prochain. We *shall decide*/
   make up our minds/take a decision next Wednesday.

Ils aimeraient que vous *vous décidiez* avant juin. They'd
   rather you *decided*/made up your mind/took a decision
   before June.


- *Se décider (à)*, can also mean 'to take a decision' or 'to
   make up one's mind'. Note that it would be possible to

replace *se décider ( à )* with *décider ( de )* in all the examples above.

## Also useful to know

*Prendre une décision* is the other way of saying 'to make/take/come to, a decision'.

# Emmener, emporter/prendre, porter, conduire – *to take someone or something, somewhere*

## Emmener

Tous les lundis j'*emmène* ma fille à la piscine. Every Monday, I *take* my daughter to the swimming pool.

Il va l'*emmener* au cinéma. He is going *to take* him/her to the pictures.

J'*ai emmené* Clémentine chez Jean-Luc. I *took* Clementine to Jean-Luc's (house).

Où vous *ont*-ils *emmené* pour votre anniversaire. Where *did* they *take* you for your birthday?

Est-ce que je peux *emmener* un ami au mariage? Can I *take* a friend to the wedding?

Ils *emmènent* toujours leurs deux chiens en vacances. They always *take* their two dogs on holiday (with them).

- *Emmener* is *to take* someone (or animals) somewhere.

## Emporter/prendre

Il faut *emporter/prendre* votre parapluie. You must *take* your umbrella.

On *emportera/prendra* un gros pique-nique. We'*ll take* a huge picnic.

Vous pouvez *emporter/prendre* ce magazine. You can *take* this magazine.

Je vais *emporter/prendre* mes jumelles. I am going *to take* my binoculars.

Il *a* tout *emporté/pris*. He *took* everything.

N'oubliez pas d'*emporter*/de *prendre* votre permis de
 conduire. Don't forget *to take* your driving licence (with
 you).

*Emporter* or *prendre* is *to take* something (with you, as
 opposed to the alternative, leaving something behind,
 implying a choice).

## Porter

Je dois *porter* l'ordonnance chez le pharmacien tout de suite.
 I must *take* the prescription to the chemist's (shop)
 straight away.

Il *a porté* son appareil au magasin parce qu'il ne marche
 plus. He *has taken* his camera to the shop because it
 doesn't work any more.

Quand *porterez*-vous les robes au pressing? When *will* you
 *take* the dresses to the drycleaners?

Vous pourriez *porter* ça à Clementine? Could you *take* that
 to Clementine?

In faut *porter* ces livres au professeur. You must *take* these
 books to the teacher.

J'ai déjà *porté* les lettres à la boîte à lettres. I *have* already
 *taken* the letters to the letter box.

Vous voulez que je *porte* le plateau dans votre chambre?
 Would you like me *to take* the tray to your room?

Elle *portera* la pellicule au magasin demain. She *will take* the
 film to the shop tomorrow.

- *Porter* is *to take* something (that you can carry) to
 someone, or somewhere for someone.

## Conduire

Il va vous *conduire* au bureau de M. Bertrand dans cinq
 minutes. He is going *to take* you to Mr Bertrand's office
 in five minutes.

Je l'*ai conduit* à la chambre d'amis. I *have taken* him/her to
 the spare room.

- *To take* someone somewhere because he/she doesn't know the way, to show the way is *conduire.*

### Also useful to know

1. **Porter** also means 'to carry' or 'to wear'.

2. **Conduire**, of course, is also 'to drive'. 'To give (someone) a lift' is **conduire**, **emmener** or **déposer en voiture** ('déposer en voiture' unlike 'conduire' and 'emmener en voiture', only means to drop someone off somewhere).

3. 'To take' the car to the garage however, is **mener** la voiture au garage.

## Faire la cuisine, cuisiner, cuire, faire cuire – *to cook*

### Faire la cuisine/cuisiner

Son mari *fait la cuisine/cuisine* tous les dimanches. Her husband *does the cooking/cooks* every Sunday.

Elle n'aime plus *faire la cuisine/cuisiner*. She doesn't enjoy *cooking* anymore.

J'étais en train de *faire la cuisine/cuisiner* quand ils sont arrivés. I was in the middle of *doing the cooking/cooking* when they arrived.

Savez-vous *faire la cuisine/cuisiner*? Can you *cook*?

Elles ne *font* jamais *la cuisine*/elles ne *cuisinent* jamais en vacances. They never *do any cooking*/they never *cook* when (they are) on holiday.

Qui va *faire la cuisine/cuisiner* pour mon anniversaire? Who is going *to do the cooking/to cook* for my birthday?

J'ai fait la cuisine/cuisiné toute la journée. I *have been cooking* all day.

- With *faire la cuisine* the emphasis is on the activity of cooking, not on what is being cooked. It is also possible to use *cuisiner.*

# Cuisiner (+ a meal/a dish)

Je *cuisinerai* votre plat préféré. *I'll cook* your favourite dish.

Savez-vous *cuisiner* un magret de canard? Can you *cook* (have you ever cooked) a duck steaklet?

Elle leur *a cuisiné* un bon repas. She *cooked* them a lovely meal.

Je vais *cuisiner* une omelette espagnole. I am going *to cook* a Spanish omelette.

Elle *avait cuisiné* le dîner pour huit heures. She *had cooked* the evening meal for eight o'clock.

On *cuisinera* un repas special. We *shall cook* a special meal.

C'est ma mère qui *a cuisiné* ce plat algérien. It's my mother who *has cooked* this Algerian dish.

- *Cuisiner* can be used to talk about *cooking* a particular meal or a particular dish.

# People + cuire/faire cuire + food(s)

Vous *cuisez/faites cuire* le poisson pendant au moins une heure. You *cook* the fish for at least one hour.

J'*ai* déjà *cuit/fait cuire* les pâtes. I'*ve* already *cooked* the pasta.

C'est un plat que l'on *cuit/fait cuire* au four. It's a dish which is *cooked* in the oven.

Nous devrons *cuire/faire cuire* beaucoup de saucisses. We shall have *to cook* a lot of sausages.

Il avait oublié de *cuire/faire cuire* les haricots verts. He'd forgotten *to cook* the green beans.

Vous n'*avez* pas assez *cuit/fait cuire* ce bifteck. You *have* under*cooked* this steak.

Je *cuirai/ferai cuire* le riz à l'avance. I'*ll cook* the rice beforehand.

Il y a eu une panne d'électricité avant que je ne puisse *cuire* le poulet. There was a power cut before I could *cook* the chicken.

- Never leave out the dish or food(s) in this key structure.

## Food(s) + cuire

Le gigot ne *cuit* que depuis une demi-heure. The joint *has* only *been cooking* for half an hour.

Ça sent bon! Qu'est-ce qui *cuit?* Lovely smell! what's *cooking?*

Cela doit *cuire* très très lentement. That has *to cook* very very slowly.

Pendant que les pommes de terre *cuisent*, je mets la table. I'm laying the table whilst the potatoes *are cooking.*

Tout *cuit* tranquillement, ce sera prêt dans dix minutes. Everything *is cooking* nicely, it will be ready in ten minutes.

- Meals, dishes or food can also be the subject of the verb *cuire.*

## Also useful to know

1. Both **préparer** or plain **faire** can be used instead of **cuisiner:** 'Je cuisinerai/préparerai/ferai un potage maison.' (I will cook/prepare/make a home-made soup).

2. **Faire des gâteaux,** or, **faire de la pâtisserie** mean **to bake** (cakes).

# Garder, s'occuper de – *to look after*

## Garder

Je veux bien vous *garder* les enfants cet après-midi. I don't mind *looking after*/keeping an eye on/watching over/ minding the children for you this afternoon.

Elle *garde* Charlie quand elle peut. She *looks after*/keeps an eye on/watch over/minds Charlie when she can.

Il lui *a gardé* le chien pendant qu'elle est entrée dans la boulangerie pour prendre le pain. He *looked after*/kept an eye on/watched over/minded the dog for her whilst she went in the bakery to get the bread.

Quand on est en vacances, nos voisins *gardent* notre

maison. Our neighbours *look after*/keep an eye on our house when we are away on holiday.

Je lui *ai gardé* le magasin ce matin. I *looked* after/minded the shop for him/her this morning.

Vous pourriez *garder* mon sac quelques minutes? Could you *look after*/keep an eye on/watch my bag for a few minutes?

Qui *gardera* les billets? Who *will look after* (have/keep) the tickets?

- *Garder* means *to look after* as in to watch over, to mind, to keep an eye on or to be in charge of people, animals or things, particularly when there is no work involved.

## S'occuper de + noun

Ma gentille voisine *s'occupera de* mes filles jeudi matin. My nice neighbour *will look after* my daughters on Thursday morning.

Elle *s'occupe* bien *de* ses vieux parents. She really *looks after* her old parents well.

Je peux *m'occuper de* ce client tout de suite, si vous voulez. I can *look after*/attend to this customer straight away, if you like.

C'est notre cousin qui *s'occupera de* notre chien lorsque nous serons en Europe. Our cousin *will look after* our dog when we are in Europe.

Vous devez *vous occuper de* madame Blanc. You must *look after* Mrs Blanc.

Martin *s'est occupé du* jardin. Martin *looked after* the garden.

Qui *s'occupe de* ce dossier? Who *is looking after* this file?

Elle a décidé de ne plus travailler, et de *s'occuper de* la maison. She has decided to stop working and *to look after* the house.

Demain il faut absolument que je *m'occupe de* tout ça. I really must *take care of* all that tomorrow.

- *To look after*, to attend to, to deal with, to take care of, to be in charge of people, animals or things (involving some work) is *s'occuper de.*

## S'occuper de + verb

Je *m'occupe de* lui téléphoner après le déjeuner. *I'll see about* phoning him/her after lunch.

Vous pourriez *vous occuper d'*acheter tout ça? Could you *see about* buying all that?

Il *s'est* enfin *occupé de* faire réparer le toit. At last he *has seen about* getting the roof repaired.

Qui s'occupera d'écrire cette lettre? Who *will see about* writing this letter?

*S'occuper de* + verb means *to see to something,* to undertake/ attend to/take care of a task.

## Also useful to know

1.  **Garder** also means 'to keep': 'Elle aimerait garder le magazine' (She would like to keep the magazine.)

2.  **S'occuper** on its own means 'to occupy oneself' or 'to busy oneself': 'Ils ne savent pas comment s'occuper pendant leur temps libre.' (They don't know how to occupy themselves in their spare time.)

3.  **Occuper** is 'to occupy': 'Je les occupe jusqu'à l'heure du souper' (I keep them occupied/busy until the evening meal.)

4.  **Être occupé** means 'to be busy' or 'to be engaged': 'Il est occupé en ce moment, je regrette' (I am afraid he is busy at the moment.)

5.  **S'occuper de ses affaires** can be the expression for 'to mind one's own business'.

# Jouir de, aimer/plaire à, profiter de, apprecier, savourer, déguster, s'amuser – *to enjoy*

## Jouir de

Je *jouis d'*une excellente santé malgré mon âge. Despite my age I (do) *enjoy* excellent health.

L'hôtel *jouit d'*une vue imprenable. Panoramic views can be *enjoyed* from the hotel.

Dans notre village nous *jouissions d'*une vie simple et tranquille. We *used to enjoy* a simple and quiet life in our village.

Le pays *jouira* ainsi *d'*une certaine prosperité économique. The country *will* then *enjoy* a degree of prosperity.

Ici, on *jouit d'*un climat doux toute l'année. Here, we *enjoy* a mild climate all the year round.

Vous devez *jouir des* beautés de la Nature. You must (should) *enjoy* the beauty of Mother Nature.

Notre médecin *a jouit d'*une excellente réputation pendant toute sa vie. Our doctor *enjoyed* an excellent reputation throughout his life.

Il ne *jouissait d'*aucun droit, et pourtant il a vendu la propriété de son grand-père. Although he (had no rights) didn't *have the benefit of* any rights whatsoever, he did sell his grandfather's property.

Dans ce camping, tout le monde pourra *jouir* de tout ce qui leur est offert, sans supplément. In this campsite, everyone will be able *to enjoy* everything that is available at no extra charge.

Ce château *jouit d'*une collection de grands tableaux. This castle *boasts* a collection of great paintings.

- *Jouir de* + noun means *to enjoy* as in to have the benefit of, or to benefit from something. Note that all the various things enjoyed when *jouir de* is used are things which are either due to nature or luck, a reward (probably earned), or a legal right.

## Aimer/plaire (à)

On *a* bien *aimé* la promenade en voiture. We *did enjoy* the car ride a lot.

Avant, j'*aimais* lire les romans policiers. I *used to enjoy* detective novels once upon a time.

Qu'est-ce qu'elles *ont* le plus *aimé* dimanche dernier? What *did* they *enjoy* the most last Sunday?

Ce film lui *a* beaucoup *plu.* He/she *enjoyed* this film very much.

Jouer au tennis leur *plaît* assez. They quite *enjoy* playing tennis.

Je pense que cela *aurait plu à* tes cousins. I think your cousins *would have enjoyed* that.

Cela me *plaisait* beaucoup. I *used to enjoy* that a lot.

- *Aimer* or *plaire (à)*, to like or to love, are two verbs which can double for *to enjoy.*

## Profiter de

Ils *ont* bien *profité de* leur escapade à Paris. They *did enjoy* their mini break in Paris.

Quand il fait beau, il faut *profiter de* son jardin. You must *enjoy*/make the most of your garden, when the weather is nice.

Mes petits-enfants *ont* bien *profité de* la piscine de l'hôtel. My grandchildren *did enjoy*/made the most of the hotel's swimming pool.

Cette femme sait vraiment *profiter de* la vie. This woman really knows how *to enjoy*/make the most of life.

- *Profiter (de)*, to take advantage (of) or to make the most (of) can double for *to enjoy.*

## Apprécier

Mes deux soeurs *apprécient* la cuisine italienne. My two sisters *enjoy*/appreciate Italian cooking.

Elle m'a dit qu'elle *avait* toujours *apprécié* sa compagnie. She told me that she *had* always *enjoyed*/appreciated his/her company.

On *a* beaucoup *apprécié* notre voyage en Europe. We *did*
*enjoy*/appreciate our trip to Europe.

Est-ce que vous *avez apprécié* le concert de Noël? *Did* you
*enjoy*/appreciate the Christmas concert?

Il n'*apprécie* pas du tout le jazz. He doesn't *enjoy* jazz at all.

• *Apprécier*, to appreciate, can double for *to enjoy*.

## Savourer

Nous venons de *savourer* une vraie bouillabaisse. We've just
*enjoyed* a real bouillabaisse.

C'est un excellent livre, franchement, je l'*ai savouré* du
début à la fin. It's an excellent book, honestly, I *enjoyed*
every page.

Maintenant, il va enfin pouvoir *savourer* son succès. At long
last, he can now enjoy the fruits of his success.

Tous les matins, pour le petit-déjeuner, ils *savourent* de
délicieux croissants au beurre. Every morning, for
breakfast, they *enjoy* delicious croissants made with
butter.

• *Savourer*, to savour, can be one other way to say *to enjoy*.

## Déguster

Nous *dégusterons* cette bouteille de champagne pour mon
anniversaire. We *shall enjoy* this bottle of champagne
for my birthday.

J'*ai dégusté* cette grande nouvelle! I really *did enjoy* this piece
of (important) news!

Ils étaient en train de *déguster* les fraises du jardin. They
were (in the middle of) *enjoying* the home-grown
strawberries.

Vanessa adore ce chanteur, elle *a dégusté* son spectacle.
Vanessa loves this singer, she couldn't *have enjoyed* his
show more.

• *Déguster*, to savour, to taste, is also another verb which can
be used to say *to enjoy*.

## S'amuser

J'espère que vous *vous amuserez* bien demain. I hope you
*enjoy yourselves* tomorrow.

Elles *s'amusent* comme ça chaque fois qu'elles viennent.
They *enjoy themselves* like this each time they come.

Tu t'*es* bien *amusé* à la boum samedi? *Did* you *enjoy* the
party on Saturday?

Ces enfants ne savent pas comment *s'amuser*. These children
don't know how *to enjoy themselves.*

Mes nièces *s'amusent* dans la piscine avec leurs copines. My
nieces *are enjoying themselves* in the swimming pool
with their friends.

Qu'est-ce qu'on *s'est amusé* chez toi hier soir! *Did* we *enjoy
ourselves* at your house last night or what!

Regarde les chiens *s'amuser* sur la plage! Look at the dogs
*enjoying themselves* on the beach!

Je ne *me suis* pas *amusée* dans cette boîte. I *did*n't *enjoy*
myself in that night club.

- *S'amuser* means *to enjoy oneself* but more as in to have a
good time, to have fun to have a good laugh.

## Also useful to know

1.  **Savourer** and **déguster** are used to translate 'to enjoy'
    mainly when talking about food or drink. With other
    things, like a book or a show, the intention is to put
    maximum stress on the verb 'to enjoy'.

2.  **S'amuser** can also mean 'to amuse oneself' and **amuser**
    someone is 'to amuse' or to 'entertain' people.

3.  **Trouver agréable** is one more way to translate 'to
    enjoy'.

4.  **Se régaler** is a more colloquial way to say 'to enjoy (a
    lot)' food, drink, time or an activity (it can replace.
    aimer, plaire, profiter, apprécier, savourer, déguster and
    s'amuser).

5. **Bon**, which probably doesn't sound strong enough in English to convey 'enjoyment', is also frequently used in parting pleasantries (enjoy + time, that is, what you are about to do next):
   - Bonne promenade. Enjoy your walk/have a nice walk.
   - Bon séjour à Dieppe. Enjoy your stay in Dieppe.
   - Bonnes vacances. Enjoy your holiday/have a nice holiday.
   - Bonne soirée. Enjoy your evening/have a nice evening.
   - Bon appétit. Enjoy your meal/have a nice meal.

6. There is one more way to say you enjoy an activity; For example, one other way to translate 'he enjoys opera' is **c'est un amateur d'opéra**. However, reverse the word order, noun+amateur (instead of amateur+noun) and the translation is quite different: 'un jardinier amateur' (an amateur gardener).

# Partir, quitter, laisser — *to leave*

## Partir

Demain, je *pars* de bonne heure. Tomorrow I *am leaving* in good time.

On partira mardi prochain, d'accord? We'll leave next Tuesday, all right?

Il faut que vous partiez tout de suite. You must leave straight away.

Quand sont-ils partis? When did they leave?

Les cars partent de la Place du Théâtre. The coaches leave (go) from the Place du Théâtre.

Tu pars déjà? Are you leaving already?

Gregory sera parti. Gregory will have left.

Le train était déjà parti. The train had already left.

- *Partir* is *to leave* as in 'to go', 'to depart'.

## Quitter

Le matin je *quitte* la maison avant mon mari. In the
    morning I *leave* home before my husband does.

Ils *ont quitté* la ville il y a au moins trois ans. They *left* the
    town at least three years ago.

Elle pourra *quitter* l'hôpital après-demain. She will be able
    *to leave* the hospital the day after tomorrow.

Je veux *quitter* cette compagnie. I want *to leave* this
    company.

Nous *avons quitté* notre amie devant le cinéma. We *left* our
    friend outside the cinema.

Il *a quitté* sa femme. He *has left* his wife.

Je l'*ai quitté* vers neuf heures. I *left* him at about nine o'
    clock.

Tout à coup elle *a quitté* le magasin. She suddenly *left* the
    shop.

- *Quitter* is *to leave* someone, or a place.

## Laisser

Ce soir, je vais *laisser* les enfants chez ma voisine. I am
    going *to leave* the children at my neighbour's this
    evening.

Je crois qu'il lui *a laissé* la clé. I believe he *left* him/her the
    key.

Est-ce qu'on peut *laisser* nos valises ici? Can we *leave* our
    suitcases here?

Qu'est-ce que vous comptez emporter, et qu'est-ce que vous
    voulez *laisser*? What do you intend to take with you,
    and what do you want *to leave* (behind)?

Il m'*a laissé* son journal. He *left* his newspaper for me.

Où *a*-t-elle *laissé* son sac? Where *did* she *leave* her bag?

Je *laisse* ça sur la table? Shall I *leave* that on the table?

Je regrette, vous ne pouvez pas *laisser* ça là. You can't *leave*
    that there, I am afraid/sorry.

Tu peux *laisser* ton sac ici. You can leave your bag here.

- *Laisser* is *to leave* someone, or to leave something
  somewhere.

### Also useful to know

1. **A partir de** means 'starting from' (a time, a date, a price or a location).

2. **Le laisser-aller** is 'carelessness', 'slovenliness'.

# Penser, croire, réfléchir, songer (à) – *to think*

## Penser

On *pense* qu'il est fort sympathique. We *think* that he is immensely nice.

*Pensez*-vous qu'elles ont tort? Do you *think* that they are wrong?

Je *pense* que cette voiture est plus confortable que l'autre. I *think* that this car is more comfortable than the other one.

Nous *avons pensé* que c'était trop cher. We *thought* that it was too expensive.

Qu'est-ce que tu *penses* du film? What do you *think* of the film?

Elle *pense* que ce serait mieux. She *thinks* that it would be better.

- *Penser* is usually *to think* as in 'to have an opinion'.

## Croire

Je *crois* qu'il va venir le onze. I *think* that he is coming on the eleventh.

On *a cru* que c'était elle. We *thought* (assumed) that it was her.

Vous *croyez* que c'est l'église de la Sainte-Mère? Do you think that this is the Sainte Mère church?

La pharmacie la plus proche? Dans la rue Leblanc, je *crois*. I think (I believe) that the nearest chemist's shop is in the rue Leblanc.

Je *crois* qu'il sait parler l'anglais et l'allemand. I *think* (I believe) that he can speak English and German.

Il *croit* que la banque ferme à cinq heures. He *thinks* that the bank closes at five.

- *Croire* is *to think* as in 'to believe', 'to assume'.

## Réfléchir

Vous n'*aviez* pas assez *réfléchi*, hein! You *had*n't *thought about* it long enough, had you!

Il va *réfléchir*. He is going *to think about* it.

It faut toujours *réfléchir* avant d'agir. You must *think* before you act.

J'ai *réfléchi*, et j'ai décidé de porter la robe bleue. I *thought about* it, and I decided to wear the blue dress.

En *réfléchissant*, je comprends maintenant. Now that I *think about* it, I do understand.

Main non, voyons, *réfléchissez* un peu! Oh come off it, *think about it*!

- *Réfléchir* is to think about something, as in 'to have a good think', 'to think hard', 'to think (something) over'.

## Songer (à)

*Songez à* vos enfants! *Think about* your children!

Il n'avait pas *songé aux conséquences*. He *had* not *thought about* the consequences.

Il faudrait *songer à* partir. We should *think about* leaving.

Ils *songent à* déménager depuis un an. They *have been thinking about* moving for one year.

*Songe* un peu *à* tous ceux qui ont moins de chance que toi! You *think about* all those who are not as lucky as you are!

J'ai *songé* longtemps *à* ça. I did *think about* that for a long time.

- *Songer à* means *to think about* as in 'to take into account/ consideration' (particularly when we mean 'don't forget...'), 'to consider', 'to muse over/upon', 'to reflect'.

## Also useful to know

1. In many cases, **penser** and **croire** are interchangeable.

2. 'To think' about someone or about something is also **penser à**: 'J'ai pensé à vous.' (I thought about you.)

3. **Penser à** things or people can also translate to **remember** something or someone or **to cross one's mind**, for example:
   - Vous croyez qu'il pensera à acheter le journal? Do you think that he will remember to buy the newspaper?
   - Tu as pensé au pain? Did you remember (to get) the bread?
   - Elle n'avait pas pensé à nous. She forgot about (taking) us (into account).
   - On n'avait pas pensé à ça. That hadn't crossed our minds.
   - J'ai pensé que ça pourrait être lui. It did cross my mind that it could be him.

4. **Réfléchir** also means 'to reflect'.

5. The ironic exclamation in English 'I don't think (so)!' is **cela/ça m'étonnerait!**

# Prendre + temps, mettre + temps – *to take time*

## Prendre son temps

Moi le dimanche, j'aime *prendre mon temps*. I like *to take my time* on Sundays.

*Prenez votre temps*, je vous en prie. Do *take your time*.

Il *a pris* tout *son temps* pour le faire. He *took* all *his time* to do it.

C'est loin mais on pourra *prendre notre temps*. It's far, but we will be able *to take our time*.

Vous *prenez* toujours *votre temps* pour répondre? Do you always *take your time* before answering?

• *Prendre son temps* means *to take one's time*.

## Prendre le temps

Je vais enfin pouvoir *prendre le temps* de lire ce gros livre.
At last, I am going to be able *to take* (have/find) *the time* to read this extremely long book.

Elle *a* toujours *pris le temps* de s'occuper de sa vieille tante.
She *has* always *taken* (had/found) *the time* to look after her old aunt.

Quand on est retraité on peut *prendre le temps* de prendre son temps. When you're retired you can *take* (have/find) *the time* to take your time.

Tu pourrais *prendre le temps* de le faire lundi prochain?
Could you *take* (find) *the time* to do it next Monday?

Il faut qu'il *prenne le temps* de tout lire. He must *take* (find) *the time* to read all of it.

Nos amis avaient gentiment *pris le temps* de nous écrire. Our friends *had* kindly *taken* (found) *the time* to write to us.

• *To take time* as in 'to have/to find the time' is *prendre le temps*.

## Things + prendre, things + prendre + people

Ce type de projet *prendra* plusieurs années. This type of project *will take* several years.

C'est un travail qui *prend* beaucoup trop de temps. It's a job which *takes* much too much time.

Normalement ce voyage *prend* combien de temps? How long does this journey usually *take*?

Cela ne *prend* jamais plus de vingt minutes. It never *takes* more than twenty minutes.

Cela *prendra* environ une heure, à mon avis. That *will take* about one hour in my opinion.

Ça *a pris* trois jours. It *took* three days.

Cela vous *prendra* seulement une demi-heure. It *will* only *take* you half an hour.

Malheureusement, ça lui *a pris* tout un jour. Unfortunately, it *took* him/her a whole day.

Cela nous *prendrait* moins de temps si nous passions par
  Rouen. It *would take* us less time if we went via Rouen.
- With these two key structures the length of time has to be
  mentioned, and the task has to be the subject of *prendre*.

# Mettre

Le train ne *met* qu'un quart d'heure. It only *takes* a quarter
  of an hour by train.
Je pense que ça ne *mettra* qu'une demi-heure. I think that it
  *will* only *take* half an hour.
Cela *a mis* des mois. It *took* months.
Ça va *mettre* trop long, non? It's going *to take* too long, isn't
  it?
Normalement ça *met* plusieurs semaines. It usually *takes*
  several weeks.
Cela *mettrait* des heures et des heures. That *would take*
  hours and hours.
Ils *ont mis* longtemps. They *took* a long time.
J'*ai mis* deux mois pour/à faire cette robe. It *took* me two
  months to make this dress.
Charlotte *mettra* moins de temps que lui. It *will take*
  Charlotte less time than him.
Combien de temps *avez*-vous *mis* pour/à laver la voiture de
  votre père? How long *did* it *take* you to wash your dad's
  car?
En voiture on *met* dix minutes environ. It *takes* us about
  ten minutes by car.
J'*ai mis* des semaines à me décider. It *took* me weeks to
  make up my mind.
Cela va me *mettre* combien de temps, à peu près? How long
  is it going *to take* me, approximately?
Ça nous *avait mis* plusieurs heures. It *had taken* us several
  hours.
Ceci leur *mettrait* des années. This *would take* them years.
Et ça vous met combien de temps en moyenne? And how
  long does it take you on average?

- *Mettre* is another choice to say *to take* time. People as well
  as tasks can be the subject of *mettre*.

## Il y en a pour, en avoir pour

Est-ce *qu'il y en a pour* longtemps/est-ce que j'*en ai pour*
   longtemps? Will it *take* long/will it *take* me a long time?
*Il y en a* pour/*j'en ai pour* trois ou quatre heures. It is going
   *to take*/me three or four hours.
*Il y en avait eu*/nous *en avions eu* pour des heures. It *had*
   *taken*/us hours.

* The two key structures above are also alternatives to
   translate *to take +time*.

## Also useful to know

1.  The key structure **people + prendre + time** means 'to
    take time off'. For example: 'Hier, j'ai pris une heure de
    plus pour le déjeuner.' (Yesterday I took one extra hour
    off for lunch.)

2.  **Avoir le temps** is 'to have time/the time'

3.  **Y mettre le/son temps** is the expression for 'to take
    one's time' as in 'to take long enough', for example: 'Eh
    bien, vous y avez mis le/votre temps!' (You took long
    enough!)

## Helping you learn

### Progress questions

1   Looking at the English side only, translate a whole section
    of one item into French and check your answers.

2   Try to listen to some French (real life conversation, course
    cassette, radio or television) until you spot one of the
    problem words/phrases/key structures.

3   Write down explanations for differences between one set
    of verbs available in French to translate one verb in English
    and check your answers.

## Discussion points

**1** Find out if your fellow students have difficulties with the same words/phrases/key structures.

**2** Never miss an opportunity to ask a native of France to explain differences you have digested, and give them the explanations!

**3** Do you agree that you never question oddity found in your mother tongue?

## Practical assignment

Discuss (and bemoan) problem words/phrases/key structures with fellow students.

## Study tips

**1** Don't wait until you can say everything in perfect French. Start using the language straight away, 'mixing' it with English if necessary.

**2** Speak in French to all willing family members and friends, yourself and your pets, and to all French people in France or in England (or other countries) at every opportunity.

# 2 **Choosing the Right Word – 1**

**One-minute overview**

Some English adverbs, adjectives and nouns have several possibilities in French. For example, *à peu près* and *environ* both mean *about* at all times. In addition some numbers can have a suffix to achieve the same result, for example *à peu près vingt*, *environ vingt* and *une vingtaine* all mean the same, *about twenty.* *Vers* normally means *towards*, but it can also be used as an alternative when talking about time, for example *vers huit heures* is the same as *à huit heures à peu près.* This chapter will show you:

- the right word for *then*
- the right word for *about*
- the right word for *half*
- the right word for *early*
- the right word for *big*
- the right word for *year, day, morning* and *evening*

## Alors, donc, puis – *then*

### Alors = à ce moment-là

Ils habitaient *alors* en Bretagne. They were *then* living in Brittany.

Elle n'avait *alors* que vingt ans. She was *then* only twenty.

Je serai *alors* toujours à Lyon. I shall still be in Lyon *then*.

Nous avions *alors* l'intention de déménager. We were *then* thinking about moving house.

C'est *alors* qu'il a tout compris. *Then* he understood everything.

Travailliez-vous *alors* pour Renault? Were you working for Renault *then*?

- *Alors* can mean *then* as in *at that time* (but, in this instance, 'then,' unlike in English, cannot be the first word of a sentence.)

## Alors = pour cette raison

Vous avez des enfants ? *Alors* vous me comprenez bien. You have children, *then* you do know what I mean.

J'y vais justement, *alors* je peux vous déposer devant la banque. I am going there, as a matter of fact, I can drop you off outside the bank, *then*.

Elle doit garder ses nièces, *alors* elle ne pourra pas venir. She has to look after her nieces, she won't be able to come *then*.

Pourquoi n'a-t-il pas téléphoné, *alors*? Why didn't he phone, *then*?

*Alors* il a fallu tout lui dire. *Then* we had to tell him/her everything.

Je dois passer devant le garage, *alors* je peux prendre de l'essence. I have to go past the garage. I can get some petrol *then*.

Ne me dites rien *alors*! Don't tell me anything *then*!

- *Alors* can also mean *then* as in *in that case* or *so, therefore, consequently*.

## Donc

Il pleut *donc* je reste ici. It's raining, I'll stay here *then*.

*Donc*, s'il n'a plus d'argent, il ne peut pas payer. He can't pay *then*, if he hasn't got any money left.

Elle n'a rien fait *donc*. She didn't do anything *then*.

Vous avez *donc* envoyé la lettre hier. You sent the letter yesterday, *then*.

Tu as oublié d'acheter le pain *donc*. You've forgotten to buy the bread *then*.

Ils n'ont pas vu Jean-Luc *donc*. They didn't see Jean-Luc *then*.

- *Donc*, just as one meaning of *alors* means *in that case, therefore, so, or, consequently*.

## Puis

Ils ont passé une semaine en Italie, *puis* une semaine en
　　Suisse. They spent one week in Italy, *then* one week in
　　Switzerland.

J'ai téléphone à Kevin, *puis* je suis sorti. I phoned Kevin,
　　(and) *then* I went out.

Vous continuez jusqu'aux feux rouges, *puis* vous tournez à
　　droite. You carry on until you get to the traffic lights,
　　*then* your turn right.

Il faut laisser cuire pendant cinq minutes, *puis* il faut ajouter
　　une cuillerée de moutarde. You have to let it cook for
　　five minutes, *then* you (need to) add one tablespoon of
　　mustard.

Elle a fait ses devoirs *puis* elle m'a aidé. She finished her
　　homework (and) *then* she helped me.

J'ai dû montrer mon passeport, *puis* remplir et signer un
　　papier. I had to show my passport, (and) *then* fill in
　　and sign a form.

- *Then* as in *next/after that/afterwards* is *puis*.

## Also useful to know

1.　**Donc** or **alors** are also frequently used at the beginning
　　or at the end of a sentence, for stress:

　　－　Vous n'avez pas d'enfants alors/donc. So, you
　　　　haven't got a family? You haven't got a family,
　　　　then?

　　－　Donc/alors, elle parle l'allemand couramment? So,
　　　　she speaks German fluently? She speaks German
　　　　fluently, then?

　　－　Entrez-donc! Do come in!

　　－　Reprenez-donc du poulet! Do have some more
　　　　chicken!

2.　The word **puis** can also mean 'furthermore' or 'besides'.
　　'Tu n'as pas le temps, puis il ne faut pas que tu négliges
　　tes études.' (You haven't got the time, furthermore/
　　besides, you must not neglect your studies.)

3.  **Puis** can also be used instead of **aussi**. 'Deux bières,
    puis une glace au chocolat, s'il vous plaît monsieur.'
    (Two beers and/and also one chocolate ice cream,
    please.)

4.  The expressions **et alors?** and **et puis après?** both mean
    'so what?'

# A peu près, environ, vers, – aine (*and* approximative-ment) – *about*

## A peu près, environ, (approximative-ment)

La pharmacie est à *environ/à peu près* cinq cents mètres de
    la gare. The chemist shop is *about* five hundred metres
    away from the station.

Elles travaillaient *environ/à peu près* quatre heures par jour
    puis elles se reposaient. They used to work about four
    hours a day, *then* they used to rest.

Notre maison a *environ/à peu près* vingt ans. Our house is
    *about* twenty years old.

Ça coûte combien *environ/à peu près*? How much is that,
    *approximately*?

Il a *environ/à peu près* cinquante cassettes. He has *about* fifty
    cassettes.

Il y avait *environ/à peu près* trente personnes derrière le
    cinéma. There were *about* thirty people behind the
    cinema.

Nous avons mis *environ/à peu près* trente minutes. It took
    us *about* thirty minutes.

Il/c'est *environ/à peu près* cinq heures. It's *about* five.

Quand nous arriverons, il sera *environ/à peu près* huit
    heures du soir. It will be *about* eight in the evening
    when we arrive.

Il était *environ/à peu près* neuf heures lorsque je l'ai vue. It
    was *about* nine when I saw her.

Il devait être *environ/à peu près* minuit. It must have been *about* midnight.

Ils terminent à *environ/à peu près* six heures. They finish at *about* six.

A quelle heure *environ/à peu près* pourrez-vous venir demain? You will be able to come at *about* what time tomorrow?

- *A peu près, environ* (and *approximativement*) are interchangeable.

## Vers

J'ai terminé le travail à environ/à peu près sept heures = J'ai terminé le travail *vers* sept heures. I finished work at *about* seven.

A quelle heure est-elle arrivée environ/à peu près? = *Vers* quelle heure est-elle arrivée? She arrived at *about* what time?

On partira à environ/à peu près midi = On partira *vers* midi. We shall leave at *about* noon.

Pierre avait commencé à environ/à peu près deux heures = Pierre avait commencé *vers* deux heures. Pierre had started at *about* two.

L'accident a eu lieu à environ/à peu près minuit = L'accident a eu lieu *vers* minuit. The accident took place at *about* midnight.

Sophie reviendra à environ/à peu près trois heures = Sophie reviendra *vers* trois heures. Sophie will come back at *about* three.

Il a téléphoné à environ/à peu près une heure = Il a téléphoné *vers* une heure. He phoned at *about* one.

- When talking about the time, if *about* can be replaced by *around*, it is also possible to used *vers*.

## Environ vingt/á peu près vingt/une vingtaine

Cela va lui coûter une cent*aine* de francs. It is going to cost him/her *about* one hundred francs.

Elle doit avoir la cinquant*aine*. She must be *about* fifty.

Elle a envoyé une vingt*aine* de lettres. She sent *about* twenty letters.

Ils seront une douz*aine*. There will be *about* twelve of them.

Nous nous connaissons depuis une trent*aine* d'années. We have known each other for *about* thirty years.

J'ai lu une diz*aine* de ses livres. I've read *about* ten of his/her books.

- To say *about* and the numbers 8, 10, 12, 15, 20, 30, 40, 50 , 60 and 100, it is also possible to add the suffix *-aine* to them (the 'x' at the end of 'dix' becomes a 'z', and final 'e's must be dropped).

However, *environ* and *à peu près* can also be used to say *about* + all numbers.

## Also useful to know

1. Une **huitaine** can mean 'about eight' but is also an alternative for 'one week'. Une **quinzaine** can mean 'about fifteen' but it can also mean 'a fortnight'. The full phrases are, respectively: une huitaine/une quinzaine de jours.

2. The word **douzaine** can have one of two meanings: 'about twelve' or 'a/one dozen.'

# Demi, moitié – *half*

## Demi

Je voudrais un kilo et *demi* de pommes de terre. I'd like one and a *half* kilos of potatoes.

Nous nous sommes promenées pendant une bonne *demi*-heure. We went for a good *half*-hour walk.

Clémentine travaille une *demi*-journée par semaine, c'est tout. Clementine works *half* a day a week, that's all.

Je crois qu'il a dix ans et *demi*. I think he is ten and a *half*.

C'est pas possible! Il est déjà trois heures et *demie*! I don't believe it! It's already *half* past three.

Je vous ai apporté une *demi*-bouteille de gin. I've brought
you *half* a bottle of gin.

Je n'en veux qu'une *demi*-livre s'il vous plaît. I only want
*half* a pound, please.

C'est quand les vacances de ce *demi*-trimestre? When is *half*-
term this term?

Deux *demi*-places pour La Rochelle. Two *half*-fares for La
Rochelle.

● *Demi* (adjective) is mainly used to translate half a standard
measure. As in English, demi + noun is just half of
something, whereas noun + demi (the opposite word
order) is one and a half something. In the latter case,
'demi' has to agree with gender of noun.

## Moitié

Tu as mangé la *moitié* du gâteau? Goinfre! You've eaten *half*
the cake? Pig!

Je n'ai lu que la *moitié* du journal. I've only read *half* the
paper.

Il a fait la *moitié* du travail hier, et l'autre *moitié* ce matin.
He did *half* the work yesterday, and the other *half* this
morning.

La *moitié* de ma famille habite en Amérique depuis dix ans.
*Half* my relations have lived in America for ten years.

On a vu la *moitié* du film français, puis nous nous sommes
couchés. We saw one *half* of the French film, then we
went to bed.

Jérôme m'a gentiment donné la *moitié* de son casse-croute.
Jerome kindly gave me *half* his snack.

Voulez-vous la *moitié* de ça? Would you like *half* of that?

C'est votre soeur qui a bu la *moitié* de la bouteille de lait.
It's your sister who drank *half* the bottle of milk.

J'avais si faim que j'ai mangé la *moitié* de la baguette. I was
so hungry that I ate *half* the baguette.

● The noun, one *half* in French is *moitié.*

### A demi – à moitié

On vient de voir un chat *à demi* mort/*à moitié* mort dans la
    rue. We've just seen a cat, *half* dead, in the street.

Pourquoi était-elle *à demi* nue/*à moitié* nue? Why was she
    *half* naked?

La porte était toujours *à demi* fermée/*à moitié* fermée. The
    door was always *half* closed.

Il doit être *à moitié* fou. He must be *half* mad.

Son lit est *à moitié* fait. His/her bed is *half* done.

Chaque fois que je le vois il est *à moitié* ivre. Each time I
    see him he is *half* drunk.

* *A demi* and *à moitié* are adverbials.

## Also useful to know

1.  The prefix **mi-** can mean 'half' as in 'part/partly'. 'Mon
    ami m'a rencontrée à mi-chemin. (My friend met me
    half way.) 'Voilà ma chambre qui fait mi-chambre mi-
    bureau.' (This is my room which is a bedroom-cum-
    study.) It can also mean 'mid-' + calendar month, for
    example **mi-avril**.

2.  The prefix **semi-** can mean 'semi', 'partly' or 'half', for
    example **semi-automatique**.

# En avance, tôt, de bonne heure – *early*

## En avance

Il faut arriver *en avance* pour l'examen. You have to arrive
    *early* for the exam.

Je n'aime pas être beaucoup *en avance* quand je vais chez le
    dentiste. I don't like being too *early* when I go to the
    dentist's.

Je suis madame Bertrand. Mon rendez-vous est à dix
    heures. Je suis un peu *en avance*. I am Mrs Bertrand.
    My appointment is at ten. I am a bit *early*.

Il préfère être *en avance*. He prefers being *early*.

Le film commence à huit heures, donc vous êtes bien *en avance*. The film starts at eight, so you are really *early*.

- *En avance* means *early* when talking about an occasion when a specified time has been arranged, is important, matters and could make a difference to situations. It could include for example the time arranged for an interview, a meeting, an appointment, a lesson, work starting time, public transport departures, etc.

## Tôt – part 1

Je suis arrivé *tôt* pour le rendez-vous. I arrived *early* for the appointment/the date.

Elle est partie *tôt* car elle avait peur de manquer son car. She left *early* because she was worried about missing her coach.

Vous êtes trop *tôt*. You are too *early*.

- *Tôt* and *en avance* can often be interchangeable.

## Tôt – part 2

Ils ne se couchent jamais très *tôt*. They never go to bed very *early*.

Le facteur est *tôt* aujourd'hui! The postman is *early* today.

J'irai en ville *tôt* demain matin. I'll go to town *early* tomorrow morning.

*Tôt* ce matin j'ai entendu un bruit dans la cuisine. *Early* this morning I heard a noise in (coming from) the kitchen.

Nous étions partis *tôt* pour arriver avant la tombée de la nuit. We had left *early* in order to arrive before it got dark.

Son anniversaire est dans deux semaines. Il est trop *tôt* pour envoyer la carte. His/her birthday is in two weeks time. It's too *early* to send the card.

J'appelle pas ça *tôt*. That's not what I call *early*/that's not *early* for me.

*Tôt* means 'early' at all other times, that is, when it does not refer to a specified time or date.

## Also useful to know

1. The opposite of **être/arriver en avance**, is **être/arriver en retard** 'to be late'.

2. **Être en retard** also means 'to be behind' (with things).

3. The opposite of **tôt** is **tard** 'late'.

4. **De bonne heure** means 'in good time'.

5. **D'avance** or **à l'avance** both mean 'in advance'.

# Grand, gros – big

## Grand – part 1

Ils n'avaient jamais vu de si *grands* pieds. They had never
  seen such *big* feet (before).
Dis donc, il est *grand* ton sac! You've got a *big* bag there!
Ils ont fait une *grande* fête. They had a *big* party.
Vous n'avez pas une boîte plus *grande* que ça par hasard?
  Would you have a *big*ger box than that one at all?
Elle m'a acheté un *grand* vase en crystal. She bought me a
  *big* crystal vase.
Je préférerais un four plus *grand*. I would rather have a
  *big*ger oven.

## Grand – part 2

On a plusieurs *grands* arbres dans notre jardin. We have
  several *big*/tall trees in our garden.
Je travaille dans le *grand* batîment à côté de la gare. I work
  in the *big*/tall building next to the station.
Vous aimeriez habiter dans un *grand* immeuble? Would you
  like to live in a *big*/tall block of flats?
Martin est assez *grand* pour son âge, n'est-ce pas? Martin is
  quite tall for his age, isn't he?

*Grand* can mean *big* as in 'tall', or indeed, it can mean 'tall'.

## Grand – part 3

J'ai une *grande* maison avec un très *grand* jardin. I have a *big* house with a very *big* garden.

C'est le pays le plus *grand* du monde. It's the *big*gest country in the world.

Ce *grand* restaurant indien est nouveau, il se trouve sur la *grande* place, au bout de la rue Blanche. This *big* Indian restaurant is new, it's on the *big* square, at the end of the Blanche street.

Quel *grand* lac! What a *big* lake!

Sa chambre n'est pas *grande*. His/her room is not *big*.

- When *big* means covering a big area, *grand* is used.

## Grand – part 4

Qu'est-ce que je vous donne, une *grande* boîte d'allumettes, ou une petite? What do I give you (what would you like) a *big* box of matches, or a small one?

La *grande* quiche fait 79 francs et celle-ci, la petite, fait 60. The *big* quiche costs 79 francs and this one, the small one, 60.

Nous avons trois tailles seulement pour les T-shirts, *grand*, moyen et petit. We only have three sizes for the T-shirts, *big* medium and small.

Alors, un panaché, deux bières, un café et un *grand* crème monsieur, s'il vous plaît. Right then, one shandy, two beers, one black coffee and one *large* white coffee please.

J'aurais dû prendre la *grande* boîte de petits pois. I should have got the *big* tin of peas.

- *Grand* can mean *big* or *large* when talking about set sizes of things.

## Grand – part 5

C'est un *grand* jour aujourd'hui. Today is a *big*/important day.

Il y a eu un *grand* repas en fin de soirée. There was a *big*/special meal at the end of the evening.

Nous venons d'apprendre votre *grande* nouvelle. We've just heard your *big*/important/great news.

C'était un *grand* docteur américain. He was a *big*/important/
  great American doctor.
Il y a eu un *grand* scandale. There was a *big* scandal.

- *Grand* can mean *big* as in 'important', 'special' or 'great'.

## Gros - part 1

Cet homme est trop *gros*. This man is too *big*/large/fat.
Devant l'école de Marie il y a plusieurs *gros* arbres, très très
  vieux. There are several very *big*/large old trees in front
  of Marie's school.
Son chat a toujours été *gros* comme ça. His/her cat has
  always been *big*/fat like that.
C'était une *grosse* femme qui aimait chanter du matin au
  soir. She was a *big*/large/fat woman who used to enjoy
  singing from morning right through the evening.

- *Gros* means 'large' or 'fat'.

## Gros – part 2

Je voudrais un kilo des *grosses* tomates. I'd like one kilo of
  the *big* tomatoes please.
Elle a acheté un *gros* poulet pour demain. She has bought a
  *big* chicken for tomorrow.
Qu'est-ce qu'ils sont *gros* ces melons, hein! My goodness,
  aren't these melons *big*!
Ce gigot n'est pas assez *gros* pour nous tous. This joint of
  lamb isn't *big* enough for us all.

- Only *gros* is used for translating *big* when talking about
  fruits and vegetables, as well as other foods where size, as
  such, has been more or less left to nature.

## Grand = gros

un grand effort: a big effort
un gros effort = un très grand effort: a very big effort

un grand orage: a big storm

un gros orage = un très grand orage: a very big storm

un grand travail: a big job
un gros travail: a massive job

une grande moustache: a big moustache
une grosse moustache: a huge moustache

une grande voiture: a big car
une grosse voiture: a big 'fat' car

un grand morceau de tarte aux pommes: a big piece of
    apple tart
un gros morceau de tarte aux pommes: a large piece of
    apple tart

un grand rhume: a big cold
un gros rhume: a filthy cold

- *Gros* can be used to make *big* bigger or stronger,
  particularly when exaggerating, or showing off.

## Also useful to know

1. **Un grand magasin** is 'a big shop' or, 'a department
   store'.
2. **Une grande personne** is 'a grown-up'.
3. **Les grandes vacances** means 'the summer holidays'.
4. **Un grand lit** is 'a double bed'.
5. **Un grand mot** is 'a big word', but **un gros mot** is 'a
   swear/rude word', and
6. **le gros lot** is 'the first prize' (in a draw).

# Un jour, une journée *(etc)* – a day *(etc)*

## Un jour, un matin, un soir, un an

Elle fait de la marche tous les *jours*, après le travail. She goes
    walking every *day*, after work.

Vous arriverez quel *jour* exactement? You will arrive on
    which *day* exactly?

Ce *matin*, je me suis occupé de mon petit frère. This
    *morning* I looked after my little brother.

Je leur ai parlé hier *matin*. I spoke to them yesterday
    *morning*.

On a décidé d'emmener notre mère et notre père au cinéma
    demain *soir*. We've decided to take our mum and dad
    to the cinema tomorrow *evening*.

Le *soir*, j'aime regarder la télévision. In the *evening*, I like
    watching television.

Ils iront en France l'*an* prochain. They will go to France
    next *year*.

L'*an* passé, je suis allée en Bretagne avec elle. I went to
    Brittany with her last *year*.

- The masculine forms, in all the examples above, are
  preferred when the emphasis is on *when* an action takes
  place.

## Number + jour (etc)

Elle les ai vus il y a deux *jours*. She saw them two *days* ago.

Je ne le connais que depuis environ dix *jours*. I have only
    known him for about ten *days*.

Jean-Luc a un chien depuis une dizaine de *jours*. Jean-Luc
    has had a dog for about ten *days*.

Sa femme travaille deux *matins* par semaine. His wife works
    two *mornings* a week.

Je fais de la marche un *matin* par semaine. I go walking one
    *morning* a week.

Vous y êtes allé trois *matins* de suite? Did you go (there)
    three *mornings* in a row?

C'est le troisième *soir* qu'il leur téléphone. This is the third
    *evening* he has phoned them.

Un *soir* la semaine prochaine, on ira chez Elise. One *evening*
    next week, we'll go to Elise's.

Trois *soirs* par mois en moyenne, ils terminaient à dix
    heures. They used to finish at ten, on average, three
    *evenings* a month.

Elle n'a que cinq *ans*. She is only *five* (years of age).

Ils ont appris le français pendant trois *ans*. They studied French for three *years*.

Voilà sept *ans* qu'ils ont divorcé. They divorced seven *years* ago.

- Again, the masculine form is preferred when day, morning, evening or year is used with a number.

## Une journée (etc)

Merci mille fois pour une *journée* très agréable. Thank you very much indeed for a very enjoyable *day*.

Vous avez eu une *journée* plutôt difficile. You've had a rather difficult *day*.

Quelle *journée* intéressante! What an interesting *day*!

J'ai passé ma *matinée* à faire le ménage. I've spent my *morning* doing the housework.

Elle s'est promenée toute la *matinée*. She went for a walk for the whole *morning*.

Ça a été une longue *matinée* pour mon père. It has been a long *morning* for my father.

On passera la *soirée* à jouer aux cartes. We shall spend the *evening* playing cards.

Je n'aime pas gaspiller mes *soirées* à regarder la télé. I don't like wasting my *evenings* watching TV.

Le pauvre, il a eu une *année* déprimante. Poor thing, he has had a depressing *year*.

Je dois dire que cela a été une *année* merveilleuse. I must say, it was a wonderful *year*.

Bonne *année* à tout le monde! Happy New *Year* to everyone!

- The feminine forms are usually used to emphasise either *how* the time is used, or to put *emphasis on the length of time*.

## Un jour (etc) = une journée (etc)

C'est mon premier jour ici = C'est ma première journée ici.

It's my first day here.

Ce sera un grand jour pour eux = Ce sera une grande journée pour eux. It will be a big day for them.

Ils ont passé un matin très intéressant = Ils ont passé une matinée très intéressante. They had a very interesting morning.

Est-ce que c'est le seul appel du matin? = Est-ce que c'est le seul appel de la matinée? Is that the only call for the morning?

Nous n'aimons pas les longs soirs d'hiver = Nous n'aimons pas les longues soirées d'hiver. We don't like the long winter evenings.

Le dernier soir, ils sont tous allés au cinéma = La dernière soirée, ils sont tous allés au cinéma. The last evening they all went to the cinema.

Ma fille apprend à conduire depuis deux bons ans = Ma fille apprend à conduire depuis deux bonnes années. My daughter has been learning to drive for two good years.

Mes parents ont l'intention d'aller en Cornouailles l'an prochain = Mes parents ont l'intention d'aller en Cornouailles l'année prochaine. My parents intend to go to Cornwall next year.

J'ai commencé il y a un an = J'ai commencé il y a une année. I started a year ago.

- Most of the time, either form can be used. However, whenever these words have a qualifying word, the feminine forms are often used. This is particularly the case for the word 'year.'

## Also useful to know

1.   One more unhelpful rule is: which form sounds better to the French!

2.   The good news, of course, is that both forms are right. Whichever form is used, it is not possible to be misunderstood.

3.   As in English, une **matinée** can also mean 'an afternoon showing' at the theatre or cinema.

# Helping you learn

### Progress questions

**1** Looking at the English side only, translate a whole section of one item into French and check your answers.

**2** Read a French passage (textbook, paper, magazine, book) and see if you can spot one of the problem words or phrases.

**3** Write down explanations for usage of each word available in French which can translate one in English and check your answers.

### Discussion points

**1** Find out if your fellow students have difficulties with the same words and phrases found in this chapter.

**2** Never miss an opportunity to ask a native of France to explain differences you have digested and give them the explanations!

### Practical assignment

Ask a fellow student to test you on material in this chapter.

### Study tips

Don't wait until you can say everything in perfect French. Start using the language straight away, 'mixing' it with English if necessary.

# Choosing the Right Word – 2

**One-minute overview**

This chapter will help you with some more problem words. For example, when *what* is before a noun, it is one of four words in French, *quel(s)* or *quelle(s)*. If *what* is not in a question it is *ce que*, but in a question it is *que* or *quoi*. *Il* can mean *it* in certain key structures, *ce* is needed to say 'what' or even 'who' *it* is, whereas *cela* (or the shortened version *ça*) translates *it* with verbs other than 'être', for example 'cela m'inquiète' (it worries me). This chapter will show you:

■ the right word for *it*
■ the right word for *both*
■ the right word for *what*

## Ce, cela, ça, il – *it (that, they)*

### Ce (c') + être + things

*C'*est son livre. *It's* his book.

*Ce* n'était pas vraiment une bonne idée. *It/that* wasn't really a good idea.

*Ce* serait le meilleur moment pour le faire. *It/that* would be the best time to do it.

*Ce* sera sans doute une longue journée. *It* will probably be a long day.

Il faut que *ce* soit une surprise. *It* has to be a surprise.

*C'*est bien le sac de Nicole? *It/that* is Nicole's bag, isn't it?

• To translate *it, that* + to be + noun, use *ce (c')*.

## Ce (c') + être + people = he, she or they

*C'*était un de mes amis anglais. *He* was one of my English friends.

*Ce* n'est pas ma belle-soeur. *She* is not my sister-in-law.

*Ce* sont les enfants de mon frère. *They* are my brother's children.

*C'*était une femme charmante. *She* was a lovely woman.

*Ce* sont mes voisins. *They* are my neighbours.

*C'*est une infirmière. *She* is a nurse.

- Quite simply, *ce (c')* is used not only to say what something is, but unlike in English, to say who *he, she* or *they* are.

## Ce (c') + être + adjective

Le français est difficile, *c'*est vrai. French is difficult, *it/that* is true.

Finir avant neuf heures, *ce* serait impossible. *It/that* would be impossible to finish before nine.

Apprendre à conduire, *c'*est maintenant indispensable. *It* is now strictly necessary to learn to drive.

Il ne faut pas refuser, *ce* serait impoli. You musn't refuse, *it/that* would be rude.

Mille fois merci pour cette soirée, *c'*etait très sympathique. Thank you ever so much for this evening, *it* was very enjoyable.

*C'*est gentil d'être venu. *It/that'*s nice of you to have come.

- When *it/that* refers back to a phrase or a sentence (statements, facts, ideas etc), use *ce (c')*.

### Il + être + adjective

*Il* ne sera pas facile de lui dire la vérité. *It* will not be easy to tell him/her the truth.

*Il* serait trop difficile pour ma mère de venir demain. *It* would be too difficult for my mother to come tomorrow.

*Il* est rare de voir vos voisins ici. *It'*s rather unusual to see your neighbours here.

*Il* est interdit de fumer dans ce restaurant. *It* is forbidden to smoke in this restaurant.

*Il* m'est facile de comprendre pourquoi il est parti. *It's* easy for me to understand why he has left.

*Il* est ridicule d'accepter. *It's* stupid to accept.

- Normally, when the main part of the sentence comes later, the impersonal 'il' is used.

# Impersonal 'il'

Il fait froid/chaud depuis trois jours. It's been cold/hot for three days.

Il y a une piscine près d'ici? Is there a swimming pool near here?

Il (vous) faut travailler. You must work.

Il vaudrait mieux rester ici. It would be better to stay here.

Il se trouve que je l'ai vu hier. It so happens that I saw him yesterday.

Il s'agit de résidences pour les personnes du troisième âge. They (/these) are homes (specially built) for old age pensioners.

Il paraît qu'elle est américaine. I've heard that she is American.

Il semble que vous ayez/Il me semble que vous avez raison. It seems/it seems to me that you are right.

Il (vous) suffit de montrer votre passeport. All you have to do is show your passport.

Il (vous) reste combien d'argent exactement? How much money is left/how much money have you got left exactly?

Il/cela/ça vous arrive d'aller au bord de la mer? Do you sometimes go to the coast?

Il/c'est presque quatre heures. It's nearly four o' clock.

- The various phrases used in these examples need the impersonal *il* except for the last two which have a choice between *il* and *cela/ça* or *ce*.

## Cela, ça + être

*C'*est vrai = *cela* est vrai (also possible: *ça* n'est pas vrai). *It/ that* is true.

*Ce* serait impossible = cela/ça serait impossible. *It/that* would be impossible.

*C'*est maintenant indispensable = *cela* est maintenant indispensable (also possible: *ça* n'est pas indispensable - *ça* lui est indispensable). *It/that* is now indispensable.

*Ce* serait impoli = *cela/ça* serait impoli. *It/that* would be rude.

*C'*était très sympa = *cela* était très sympa (also possible: *ça* n'était pas très sympa). *It/that* was very friendly.

*C'*est gentil = *cela* est gentil (also possible: *ça* n'est pas gentil). *It/that* is kind.

- It is also possible to use *cela* or *ça* in place of *ce*, except when 'est' (is) or 'était' (was) is the next word after 'ça' (most probably because it would be awkward to say).

## Cela, ça + other verbs (including auxiliary verbs)

*Ça* a été une matinée plutôt difficile. *It* has been a rather difficult morning.

*Cela* avait été une grande decision. *It* had been an important decision.

*Ça* aurait été une question intéressante. *It* would have been an interesting question.

*Cela* aura été son choix. *It* will have been his/her choice.

*Cela* vous va bien. *It/that* does suit you.

*Ça* ne se fait pas! *It/that* isn't done!

*Ça* fait combien? How much does *it* come to?

*Cela* ne fait rien. *It/that* doesn't matter.

*Ça* s'est passé devant la gare. *It/that* happened outside the station.

Est-ce que *cela* vous conviendrait? Would *it/that* suit you?

*Ça* dépend. *It/that* depends.

Qu'est-ce que *cela* veut dire? What does *it/that* mean?

*Cela* ne nous a jamais intéréssés. *It/that* has never interested us.

- *Cela* or *ça* are used to translate *it* or *that* with all other verbs as well (except when 'est' or 'était' is the next word after ça, most probably because it would be difficult to say).

## Also useful to know

1. There are two slightly different ways to state someone's occupation: 'C'est un boulanger = Il est boulanger.' (He is a baker.')

2. **Ceci**, 'this' could replace **cela/ça** 'that': 'ceci ne nous a jamais interessés' (this has never interested us).

3. **Cela**, **ça** and **ceci** can of course be the object of a sentence. 'Je n'aime pas cela/ça/ceci.' (I don't like that/this.) 'Qui a fait cela/ça/ceci?' (Who did that/this?)

# Les deux, tous les deux, tous deux, à la fois – *both*

Les deux/tous les deux/tous deux

*Les deux* chapeaux lui vont vraiment bien = Les chapeaux lui vont vraiment bien *tous les deux*. Both (the) hats really suit him/her.

*Les deux* lui vont vraiment bien = *Tous deux* lui vont vraiment bien. They *both* suit him/her.

*Les deux* livres étaient sur la table = Les livres étaient sur la table, *tous les deux*. Both (the) books were on the table.

*Les deux* étaient sur la table = *Tous deux* étaient sur la table. They were *both* on the table.

*Ces deux* dames ont demandé un dépliant = Ces dames ont demandé un dépliant *toutes les deux*. Both these ladies asked for a leaflet.

*Les deux* ont demandé un dépliant = *Toutes deux* ont demandé un dépliant. They *both* asked for a leaflet.

*Les deux* amis de Richard iront à l'université en septembre = Les amis de Richard iront à l'université en septembre, *tous les deux*. Both Richard's friends will go to university in September.

*Les deux* iront à l'université en septembre = *Tous deux* iront à l'université en septembre. Both will go to university in September.

*Les deux* compagnies nous ont répondu = Les compagnies nous ont répondu, *toutes les deux*. Both companies replied.

*Les deux* nous ont répondu = *Toutes deux* nous ont répondu. *Both* replied.

*Les deux* sacs sont beaucoup trop chers = Les sacs sont beaucoup trop chers, *tous les deux*. Both (the) bags are too expensive.

*Les deux* sont trop chers = *Tous deux* sont trop chers. They are *both* too expensive.

*Les deux* enfants de Pierre me connaissent depuis au moins trois ans = Les enfants de Pierre me connaissent depuis au moins trois ans, *tous les deux*. Both Pierre's children have known me for at least three years.

*Les deux* me connaissent depuis au moins trois ans = *Tous deux* me connaissent depuis au moins trois ans. *Both* have known me for at least three years.

*Les deux* tableaux me plaisent énormément = Les tableaux me plaisent énormément, *tous les deux*. I like *both* the pictures immensely.

*Les deux* me plaisent énormément = *Tous deux* me plaisent énormément. I like *both* of them immensely.

*Les deux* élèves ont quitté l'école vers cinq heures = Les élèves ont quitté l'école vers cinq heures, *tous les deux*. *Both* the pupils left school at about five.

*Les deux* ont quitté l'école vers cinq heures = *Tous deux* ont quitté l'école vers cinq heures. *Both* left school at about five.

*Les deux* clients sont tout à fait d'accord avec moi = Les clients sont d'accord avec moi, *tous les deux*. *Both* the customers agree with me.

*Les deux* sont d'accord avec moi = *Tous deux* sont d'accord avec moi. *Both* agree with me.

*Les deux* chiens de ma grand-mère sont malades = Les chiens de ma grand-mère sont malades, *tous les deux*. *Both* my grandmother's dogs are ill.

*Les deux* sont malades = *Tous deux* sont malades. *Both* are ill.

Je ne savais pas que *les deux* Espagnols travaillaient ici = Je
    ne savais pas que les Espagnols travaillaient ici, *tous les
    deux*. I didn't know that *both* Spanish men worked
    here.
Je ne savais pas que *les deux* travaillaient ici = Je ne savais
    pas que *tous deux* travaillaient ici. I didn't know that
    they *both* worked here.

- For people and things, it is possible to use *les deux, tous/toutes
  les deux, tous/toutes deux* to say the same thing although, as
  the examples show, each key structure is slightly different.

## A la fois

C'est une idée *à la fois* absurde et dangereuse. It's *both* a
    stupid and dangerous idea.
Aujourd'hui j'ai *à la fois* froid et chaud! Je dois couver
    quelque chose. I am *both* hot and cold today! I must be
    sickening for something.
Excellente escapade! On s'est *à la fois* reposé et amusé.
    Excellent mini-break! We rested and had fun, *both*.
Ce tableau est *à la fois* émouvant et comique. This picture is
    *both* moving and funny.
Ils ont fait les deux *à la fois*. They did *both*.

- *Both* + two adjectives/past participles or *both* + two verbs is *à
  la fois*.

## Also useful to know

Like **en même temps** the literal translation of **à la fois** is 'at
the same time,' so it could be used for more than two
things as well:

- – Franchement, je pense que c'est une idée à la fois
    égoïste, insensée et dangereuse. I honestly think
    that it is a selfish, insane and also dangerous idea.
- – Moi, je ne peux pas faire tout à la fois. I can't do
    everything at once.

# Quel(s)/quelle(s), que, quoi, ce que, ce qui – *what*

## Quel(s), quelle(s)

*Quel* courage! *What* courage!

*Quel* jour vous convient? *What*/which day suits you?

A *quelle* heure quittez-vous le bureau d'habitude? At *what* time do you normally leave the office?

*Quelle* sera votre adresse? *What* will your address be?

*Quels* journaux lisent-ils? *What* newspapers do they read?

*Quelles* oranges voulez-vous, les plus grosses? *Which* oranges would you like, the bigger ones?

- *What* + noun is *quel(s)* or *quelle(s)*

## Que (qu')

*Qu'*est-ce que cela veut dire exactement? *What* does it/this mean exactly?

*Que* cherchez-vous monsieur? *What* are you looking for, sir?

*Qu'*est-ce qu'il y avait à faire et à voir là-bas? *What* was there to do and to see over there?

*Que* diront-elles? *What* will they say?

*Qu'*auriez-vous fait à ma place? *What* would you have done in my place?

*Qu'*avait-il acheté? *What* had he bought?

- When *what* + subject and verb is in a question, use *que*.

## Quoi

Il a vu *quoi*? = *Qu'*est-ce qu'il a vu? = *Qu'*a-t-il vu? *What* did he see?

Vous ferez *quoi* pendant les grandes vacances? = *Qu'*est-ce que vous ferez pendant les grandes vacances? = *Que* ferez-vous pendant les grandes vacances? *What* will you do during the summer holiday?

Elles voulaient *quoi*? = *Qu'*est-ce qu'elles voulaient ? = *Que* voulaient-elles? *What* did they want?

Leur fille achètera *quoi*? = *Qu'*est-ce que leur fille achètera?

= *Qu'*achètera leur fille? *What* will their daughter buy?

Vous diriez *quoi*? = *Qu'*est-ce que vous diriez? = *Que* diriez-vous? *What* would you say?

- As illustrated, when the interrogative form used is not the addition of 'est-ce que' or the reversing of subject and verb, not only the word *what* has to be at the end of the question but it becomes *quoi*.

## Ce que

Voilà *ce qu'*il a acheté. Here is *what* he bought.

Ce n'est pas du tout *ce que* j'ai compris. That's not *what* I understood at all.

Ils ne savaient pas *ce qu'*elle voulait. They didn't know *what* she wanted.

Charlotte fait toujours *ce qu'*elle veut, de toutes façons. Charlotte always does *what* she likes, anyway.

*Ce que* nous aimons le plus regarder à la télé, c'est le feuilleton australien. *What* we love watching on TV most of all is the Australian soap.

Quand j'ai su *ce qu'*il avait fait, j'ai pleuré. When I heard about *what* he had done, I cried.

- When *what* is not in a question, *ce que* is used.

## Ce qui

Ce n'est pas *ce qui* sera le plus important. That's not *what* will be the most important thing.

On ne m'a pas dit *ce qui* a été dit à la réunion. They didn't tell me *what* was said at the meeting.

*Ce qui* m'inquiète, c'est qu'il ne le sait pas encore. *What* worries me is that he doesn't know yet.

Je pense que c'est *ce qui* la surprendra un peu. In my opinion, that's *what* will surprise her a little.

*Ce qui* lui a coûté beaucoup d'argent, c'est le logement. Accommodation is *what* cost him/her a lot of money.

Voici *ce qui* se passe tous les mois. This is *what* happens every month.

- *Ce qui* is *what*, when *what* is the subject of the following verb.

## Also useful to know

1. After a preposition (including prepositions which always follow certain verbs) only **quoi** can be used:

    - De quoi s'agit-il monsieur? What is it about, sir?
    - Avec quoi fait-on ce plat? What do you need in order to make this dish?
    - Derrière quoi avez-vous laissé vos bagages? You left your luggage behind what?
    - De quoi leur parlerons-nous? What shall we talk to them about?

2. Sometimes **Ce qui** can also mean 'which' or 'that': 'Ce qui veut dire quoi?' (Which means what?) 'Il a mangé tout ce qui restait dans le frigidaire.' (He ate all that was left in the fridge.)

## Helping you learn

### Progress questions

1. Looking at the English side only, translate a whole section of one item into French and check your answers.

2. When listening to, or reading in the language, concentrate on usage of these problem words.

3. Write down explanations for when to use what and check your answers.

### Discussion points

1. Find out if your fellow students have difficulties with the same words and phrases.

    How are all skills learned?

2. Why should speaking a foreign language be different?

## Practical assignment

Listen to a French radio station as often as possible.

## Study tips

**1** Write something in French every day, even if only personal lists (shopping, things to do, etc) or, when possible, short messages.

**2** The only 'secret' of achieving fluency is practice.

**Sorry and I Don't Mind**

To say *sorry* in French, it is possible to say *pardon, désolé, je regrette* and more, but you might wish to know how to be more emphatic for more specific occasions, such as when hearing really bad news. On another topic, *I don't mind* can be *cela m'est égal* when it means *it doesn't make any difference to me, je veux bien* (said without enthusiasm) or *cela ne me dérange pas* if you want to say either *it isn't a problem for me,* or, *I couldn't care less.* This chapter will show you:

■ numerous examples which illustrate subtle differences

■ the best use of each word or phrase to say what you mean

■ how to avoid misunderstandings and upsets

■ a short cut to speed and perfect your fluency in French

## Ça m'est égal, je veux bien, ça ne me dérange pas – *I don't mind*

### Ça m'est égal

Q. On va au cinéma jeudi ou vendredi soir? A. *Ça m'est égal.*

Q. Shall we go to the pictures on Thursday or Friday evening? A. *I don't mind (which).*

Q. Tu veux un thé ou un café? A. *Ça m'est égal.*

Q. What would you like, tea or coffee? A. *I don't mind.*

Q. A quelle heure voulez-vous manger ce soir? A. *Ça nous est* tout à fait *égal.*

Q. At what time would you like to eat tonight? A. *We* really *don't mind.*

- When a choice is offered, *ça m'est égal* is the best way to translate *I don't mind* (it doesn't make any difference to me.)

## Je veux bien

Q. Si on allait à la plage demain? A. Oui, *je veux bien*.

Q. What about going to the beach tomorrow? A. *I don't mind*.

Q. Tu viens avec moi en ville la semaine prochaine? A. *Je veux bien*, moi.

Q. Do you want to come shopping with me next week? A. Yes all right, *I don't mind*.

Q. On prend des pizzas pour ce soir? A. *Je veux bien*, d'accord.

Q. Shall we get some pizzas for tea/dinner? A. OK, *I don't mind*.

- When a suggestion for plans is made, *je veux bien*, said without enthusiasm, is the best way to translate *I don't mind* (said enthusiastically it will mean: that would be great!)

## Cela/ça ne me dérange pas

Q. Pourriez-vous me poster cette lettre en allant aux magasins? A. Oui bien sûr, *ça ne me dérange pas* du tout.

Q. Could you post my letter on your way to the shops? A. Yes of course! *I don't mind* at all.

Q. Pardon Madame, je peux mettre mon manteau sur ce siège (a free seat near you on a coach)? A. Oui, *ça ne me dérange pas*, hein.

Q. Excuse me, may I leave my coat on this seat? A. Please do, *I don't mind*.

Q. *Cela vous dérangerait* que je vienne une heure plus tard demain? A. Pas du tout.

Q. Would you mind if I came one hour later tomorrow? A. Not at all.

*Ça ne me dérange pas* is the best way to say *I don't mind* (it's no trouble, no problem) in answer to a (usually small) favour.

## Also useful to know

1. **Ça m'est égal** can also mean 'I don't care/I couldn't care less', for example: 'Ça m'est égal qu'il ne me parle plus.' (I couldn't care less if he doesn't speak to me anymore.)

2. Non-verbal communication, that is, tone of voice, facial expressions and gestures, plays a big part in conveying which meaning is intended.

3. **Je veux bien** is also the phrase which can translate 'I can understand/accept that.'

4. When people apologise because of a slight problem, there is another phrase which can mean 'I don't mind/never mind/it doesn't matter/don't worry about it/it's all right/no problem', and which can double for **pas de problème**. It is **c'est (ce n'est) pas grave**. You can use it, for example, in answer to someone who apologises for being a bit late, or for forgetting to do something for you etc.

5. **Tant pis** means 'never mind/it doesn't matter' as well as 'too bad.'

# Pardon/excusez-moi, je m'excuse, désolé, je regrette – *sorry*

## Pardon, excusez-moi

- To attract a stranger's attention before asking for some simple information (the way to somewhere, the time of the day etc) use *pardon/excusez-moi*: 'Pardon/excusez-moi madame, vous connaissez la Pizzeria Tino par hasard?' (Excuse me, do you know the Pizzeria Tino at all?)

- *Pardon* or *excusez-moi* can be used to get the attention of waiters and waitresses, or the attention of staff who are there to help. The alternative here is to call: 'Monsieur (or madame) s'il vous plaît!'

- To say *sorry* when apologising for a minor accident (dropping something, bumping into someone), or when apologising for making mistakes (someone's name, the wrong drink order etc) is also *pardon* or *excusez-moi*.

- Use *pardon* also when you would like someone to repeat something because you didn't hear or understand something.

## Désolé(e)

Je suis *désolé* monsieur, il n'y a plus de pain. I am *sorry*, there is no bread left.

Je ne sais pas où se trouve la poste, *désolé*. I don't know where the post office is, *sorry*.

Il ne pourra pas venir, il est vraiment *désolé*. He is really *sorry* that he won't be able to come.

- *Désolé(e)* usually means that you are *sorry* that you cannot oblige or help someone, usually through no fault of your own.

## S'excuser (de)

Il *s'est excusé d'*arriver si tard. He *apologized* for arriving so late.

Je *m'excuse de* vous couper. *Sorry* to interrupt you (I apologise for interrupting you).

Il faudra *vous excuser*. You will have *to apologise*.

Nous *nous excusons de* vous déranger. *Sorry* to disturb you (we apologise for disturbing you).

- *S'excuser (de)* is *to apologise* for making a mistake, or doing something that puts someone out.

## Regretter (de)

Je *regrette* énormément *d'*avoir dit ça. I am really very *sorry* I said that/I really regret saying that.

Ils *regretteront* toujours *d'*y avoir été. They will always be *sorry* that they went (there)/They will always regret going (there).

Je *regrette* monsieur, il n'y a plus de places dans le car. There are no seats left on the coach, very *sorry*/I am afraid there are no seats left on the coach.

Je *regrette* mais les photocopies ne sont pas gratuites. The photocopies are not free, *sorry*/I am afraid the photocopies are not free.

- *Regretter (de)* means *to be sorry* often for causing disappointment, or, to regret. It can be used to translate 'I am afraid'.

## Etre navré (de)

Nous *avons été* vraiment *navrés d'*apprendre cette triste nouvelle. We *were very sorry* to hear this sad news.

Nicole *est navrée d'*avoir fait tant de peine à ses parents. Nicole *is really sorry* to have upset her parents so much.

Je *suis navré* mais vous n'avez rien gagné madame! I *am so sorry*, you have not won anything!

- *Navré* means *very sorry*, or *sorry and sad* or *upset*. It is probably the strongest way to say sorry.

## Also useful to know

1. The differences between these various ways of saying sorry are very subtle. Therefore, in many instances **désolé, s'excuser, regretter**, and **être navré** could be interchangeable.

2. **Demander pardon de,** or just **pardon de** means 'to ask to be forgiven': 'Je vous demande pardon d'/pardon d'avoir oublié votre anniversaire.' (Sorry, I forgot/forgive me for forgetting your birthday.)

3. **Pardonner** means 'to forgive': 'Il ne lui a jamais pardonné.' (He never forgave him/her.)

# Helping you learn

## Progress questions

Write down the subtle differences between phrases discussed in this chapter, and check your explanations.

## Discussion points

1. How important are subtle differences in language for avoiding misunderstandings, disappointments or upsets?

2. Knowing when to use what could mean a more enjoyable time in the country.

## Practical assignment

Try to spot which phrase is used when, in real life situations, or study cassettes, radio, television (especially in films).

## Study tips

1. Use all the French you know at every opportunity.

2. Learning a foreign language is just learning a skill, which, just as in your own language, can be extended throughout life.

For example, *là* can double for *here* or *there* but it has a number of other uses. *On* literally means *one* (third person singular subject pronoun), but it is also used a great deal in conversation to translate a plural subject, such as *we, they* or *people*. *Passer* can mean *to pass something, to go past, to spend* (time) and much more. This chapter will show you:

- all the uses of *là*
- all the uses of *on*
- most uses of *passer*
- which words translate *to stay*, when and why
- the actual translations of *s'agir de*

# Là or y – *there*

## Y or là

Quand je suis retournée dans la chambre la valise n'*y* était plus/la valise n'était plus *là*. When I got back to the room, the suitcase wasn't *there* any more.

Je suis allée à la piscine et Roxane *y* était aussi/était *là* aussi. I went to the swimming pool and Roxane was also *there*.

Q.　Elles sont bien nées en Norvège? They were born in Norway, weren't they?

A.　En effet, elles *y* sont nées/elles sont nées *là* en 1965. Indeed, they were born *there* in 1965.

Q.　Vous aimez habiter à la campagne? Do you enjoy living in the country?

A.　J'aime beaucoup *y* habiter/J'aime beaucoup habiter *là*. I love living *there*.

Q. Ils travaillent à la gare? Do they work at the station?

A. Ils *y* travaillent tous les deux/Ils travaillent *là* tous les deux. They both work *there*.

Q. Elle va souvent chez sa grand-mère? Does she often go to her grandmother's?

A. Elle *y* passe deux semaines tous les étés/Elle passe deux semaines *là* tous les étés. She spends two weeks *there* every summer.

Q. Le sac n'est pas dans la voiture? Isn't the bag in the car?

A. Non, il n'*y* est pas/il n'est pas *là*. It's not *there*.

Q. Elle est en Belgique depuis longtemps? Has she been in Belgium for a long time?

A. Elle *y* est depuis trois jours/Elle est *là* depuis trois jours. She's been *there* three days.

Q. Il est resté à l'hôpital combien de temps? How long did he stay in hospital for?

A. Il *y* est resté/Il est resté *là* un mois. He stayed *there* one month.

Q. Les chiens sont dans le jardin? Are the dogs in the garden?

A. Ils n'*y* sont plus/Ils ne sont plus *là*. They're not *there* any more.

Q. Est-ce qu'ils vont toujours sur la Côte d'Azur? Do they always go to the French Riviera?

A. Ils *y* vont toujours/Ils vont toujours *là*. They always go *there*.

- *Y* and *là* both mean *there* when it replaces an expression of place previously mentioned. In some cases, the place is only implied but definitely clear between interlocutors. Although they are interchangeable in the examples above, *là* would be used in more informal conversation, and in exams, *y* would be preferred.

## Là

Il n'est pas encore *là*. He is not *there/here*. (He hasn't arrived yet).

Ils sont *là*. (when back from wherever). They're *there/here*. (They're back/home/in.)

Je suis *là*, dans le salon! I am *here/over here*, in the lounge!

Allô, je voudrais parler à Caroline, elle est *là*? Hello (on the phone), I'd like to talk to Caroline. Is she *there/here* (is she in)?

Est-ce que le courrier est *là*? Is the post *there/here*? (Has the post arrived?)

Vous mangez *là*, ça me fait plaisir. Do eat *here*, that would be nice (Please do stay for lunch/dinner.)

C'est son chien qui l'a sauvée. Sans lui elle ne serait plus *là*. She was saved by her dog. She wouldn't be *there/here* (she wouldn't be alive today) but for him.

- *Là* can be the word to use when *there* or *here* really refer to a physical presence.

## Là, or ici

Valerie travaille toujours *là/ici*. Valerie still works *there/here*.

Heureusement que tu es *là/ici*. Thank goodness you're *there/here*.

Le courrier est *là/ici*, sur la table basse. The post is *there/here*, on the coffee table.

Il mangera *là/ici*. He will eat *there/here*.

Tu seras sans doute *là/ici* à quatre heures. You'll probably be *there/here* at four.

Assieds-toi *là/ici*. Sit *there/here*.

Signez *là/ici*, je vous prie. Please sign *there/here*.

La salle de bains, est *là/ici*. The bathroom is *there/here*.

Vous cherchez la gare? Elle est *là/ici*. You're looking for the station? It's *there/here*.

Roxane est *là/ici*, regarde! Roxane is *there/here*, look!

- Depending on the context, *là* can be translated with either '*there*', or, '*here*' when it is an alternative to *ici*. Also, when pointing at things or people, *là* means *there* and *ici* is *here*.

## Also useful to know

1. **Là** is a word which is a big favourite as an extra noise at the beginning, in the middle or at the end of sentences. For example:
   - Là, nous lui avons dit ce que nous pensions! Well, we told him/her what we thought!
   - On a fait un pique-nique sur la plage, là hein, comme hier. We picnicked on the beach, you know, same as yesterday.
   - Vous pouvez pas faire plus attention là. Can you be more careful, honestly!

2. The following two key structures show how it is also possible to use *là* or *ici* as well as 'où' when in English we would only need 'where':
   - C'est où il étudie tous les soirs = C'est là/ici qu'il étudie tous les soirs. It/this/that is where he studies every evening.
   - C'est où vous avez rencontré votre mari? = C'est là/ici que vous avez rencontré votre mari? Is it/this/that where you met your husband?
   - Ce n'est pas où ma mère est née = Ce n'est pas là/ici que ma mère est née. It/this/that is not where my mother was born.
   - C'est où ils jouent pendant les vacances = C'est là/ici qu'ils jouent pendant les vacances. It/this/that is where they play during the holidays.
   - C'est pas où Stéphanie travaille? = C'est pas là/ici que Stéphanie travaille? Isn't it/this/that where Stephanie works?

# On = nous etc – *one*

## We

*On* a trois enfants=*Nous* avons trois enfants. *We* have three children.

*On* lui téléphonera un jour=*Nous* lui téléphonerons un jour. *We*'ll phone him/her one day.

*On* ne parle pas bien anglais=*Nous* ne parlons pas bien anglais. *We* do not speak English very well.

*On* avait mangé des croissants=*Nous* avions mangé des croissants. *We*'d had croissants to eat.

*On* est arrivé en retard=*Nous* sommes arrivés en retard. *We* arrived late.

*On* aurait acheté une autre voiture=*Nous* aurions acheté une autre voiture. *We* would have bought another car.

*On* va à la piscine deux fois par semaine=*Nous* allons à la piscine deux fois par semaine. *We* go to the swimming pool twice a week.

- The literal translation of *on*, the subject pronoun, is *one*. One reason which makes *on* difficult to get used to is that, despite its literal translation, it is nearly always used as a plural subject. Using *one* in English in everyday conversation usually sounds formal, funny or perhaps silly. In French this is never ever the case. *On* is used continually in place of *nous* by the French, and the former actually sounds less formal than the latter.

## You (people), they (people), people, some people

*On* ne peut pas se garer ici. *You* can't park here.

*On* crie dehors. *Some people* are screaming outside.

En France *on* mange beaucoup de pain. In France, *you/they/ people/we* eat a lot of bread.

*On* me regarde. *People* are looking at me.

*On* ne parle pas avec la bouche pleine. *You* don't speak with your mouth full.

*On* se pose beaucoup de questions depuis sa démission. Since his/her resignation, *people* have had a lot of unanswered questions.

*On* ne l'a pas compris. *Some people* didn't understand him.

- When the subject could be vague, less direct, or unknown *on* is very useful.

## Someone/anyone

Est-ce qu'*on* veut me voir? Does *someone/anyone* want to see me?

*On* peut m'aider le mois prochain. *Someone* can help me next month.

*On* a laissé ce livre sur cette table. *Someone* has left this book on this table.

*On* a touché à mes affaires. *Someone* has touched my things.

*On* a cassé une tasse. *Someone* has broken a cup.

*On* sonne. There is *someone* at the door (ringing the doorbell).

- Another translation of *on* can be *someone* or *anyone*, in place of 'quelqu'un'.

## I

*On* vous apporte ça tout de suite monsieur (your order, in a café, for example)=Je vous apporte ça tout de suite. *I*'ll bring that for you straight away, sir.

*On* ne va pas bien aujourd'hui=Je ne vais pas bien aujourd'hui. *I* am not very well today.

*On* ne savait pas qu'il faut composter le billet=Je ne savais pas qu'il faut composter le billet. *I* didn't know that I have to stamp/punch the (train) ticket.

Vous ouvrez le capot, et *on* va regarder ça (car troubles at the garage)=Vous ouvrez le capot et je vais regarder ça. Open the bonnet please and *I*'ll have a look (at it).

- *On* is not very often used to replace 'je'. When it is, it is usually in order to feel less conspicuous or less responsible.

## Also useful to know

1. In French the active voice, using *on* as the subject, is often preferred to the passive voice, for example:
   - On lui a donné de l'argent=De l'argent lui a été donné. He/she was given some money.
   - On a emmené Chloë au cinéma pour son anniversaire = Chloë a été emmenée au cinéma

pour son anniversaire. Chloë was (has been) taken to the pictures for her birthday.

– On les présentera=Ils seront présentés. They will be introduced.

– On m'a vu=J'ai été vu. I was seen.

– On nous a demandé nos noms=Nos noms nous ont été demandés. We were asked our names.

2.   Note that an untranslatable 'l' can be added before **on** after the words si - où - et - que (when not only the unnecessary 'l' often makes the sentence easier to say, but it also often sounds more elegant), for example:

– Je me demande si l'on me comprend vraiment. I wonder if you/people/they understand me.

– C'est un endroit où l'on se sent complètement libre. It's a place where one/we/you/people/they/I feel completely free.

C'est un plat que l'on/qu'on mange froid. You/we/they/people eat this dish cold.

# Passer – *many meanings*

## Passer, something to someone

Vous pourriez me (faire) *passer* la moutarde? Could you *pass* me the mustard?

Je te *passerai* le journal dans cinq ou dix minutes. I'll *give* you/let you have the newspaper in five or ten minutes.

Elle leur a *passé* la serviette. She *passed* the towel over to them/she let them have the towel.

Pouvez-vous faire *passer* le pain? Could you *pass* the bread around?

Il ne veut pas me *passer* le stylo. He doesn't want *to pass* the biro over/he doesn't want to give me/let me have the biro.

•   *Passer* means *to pass, to pass over* as in 'to let someone have something'.

## Passer, a place, or, someone

Une fois que vous *avez passé* l'hôtel de ville, vous tournez à
droite. Once you *have gone past* the town hall, turn
right.

Le car *passe* bien devant la cathédrale? The coach does *go
past* the cathedral, doesn't it?

Chrystelle avait décidé de *passer* par Lyon. Chrystelle had
decided *to go through* (via) Lyon.

*Avons*-nous *passé* la frontière? *Have* we *gone past* (crossed)
the border?

Il les *a passés* ce matin dans le couloir. He *passed* them this
morning in the corridor.

Je viens de *passer* Henri. I've just *passed* Henri.

- *Passer* can mean *to go past* something or someone.

## Passer, somewhere

Je peux facilement *passer* à la pharmacie avant de rentrer ce
soir. I can easily *drop in* at the chemist's shop on my
way home tonight.

Ils *passeront* chez Nicole vers dix heures, je crois. They *will
call on* Nicole at about ten, I believe.

Elle *est passée* il y a dix minutes, tout juste. She *dropped by*
no more than ten minutes ago.

On doit *passer* la voir dans trois jours. We are due to *call on*
her in three days' time.

- *Passer* somewhere means *to drop in/by, to call on/in/at.*

## Passer prendre/chercher things, or people

Elle pourra sans doute *passer* les *prendre/chercher* lundi
prochain. She will probably be able *to fetch* them next
Monday.

Mon fils *passe* me *prendre/chercher* tous les dimanches. My
son comes *to fetch* me every Sunday.

Il faut que je *passe prendre/chercher* mon courrier. I have *to
collect* my post.

On *est passé* la *prendre/chercher* à cinq heures, comme prévu.
We *picked* her *up* at five as arranged.

- Both the phrases *passer prendre* and *passer chercher* mean *to fetch, to pick up* or *to collect* things or people.

## Passer + time

Il *a passé* toute la matinée au lit. He *spent* the whole morning in bed.

Je *passe* beaucoup de temps dans mon jardin. I *spend* a lot of time in my garden.

Ils vont *passer* une quinzaine à Marseille. They are going *to spend* a fortnight in Marseilles.

Où *passerez*-vous Noël? Where *will* you *spend* Christmas?

Elle *passe* trop de temps chez eux. She *spends* too much time at their house.

- *Passer* + time means *to spend* (time).

## Passer + an exam

Quand est-ce que votre ami va *passer* son permis de conduire? When is your friend going *to take* his driving test?

Elles *passeront* leur bac l'année prochaine. They *will take*/sit their bac next year.

Pour devenir vétérinaire, il faut *passer* beaucoup d'examens. To become a vet you have *to take* many exams.

Il ne l'a pas réussi, alors il a l'intention de le re*passer* l'année prochaine. He didn't pass, so he intend *to take* it again next year.

- *To take*, to sit an exam is *passer*.

## Se passer

On ne m'a pas dit ce qui *s'est passé*. They haven't told me what *has happened*.

Cela *se passe* toujours après minuit. That always *happens* after midnight.

Que *se passera*-t-il? What *will happen?*

Voici ce qui *se passerait.* This is what *would happen.*

Où est-ce que cela *se passe* normalement? Where does it *take place,* normally?

- *Se passer* means to happen, *to take place.*

## Se passer de + things or people

Ils n'ont nullement l'intention de *se passer de* vacances cette année. They have no intention whatsoever *to go without* a holiday this year.

Moi, je *me passe* facilement *de* la télévision. I can easily *do without* the television.

Vous *vous* en *passerez,* puisqu'il n'y en a plus. You'*ll do without* it since there isn't any left.

On *se passera de* lui. We'*ll manage without* him.

Je ne peux pas *me passer de* vous. I cannot *manage without* you.

- *Se passer de* + things or people. *To go/do/manage without.*

## Also useful to know

1. **Aller chercher/prendre** 'go and pick up/fetch/collect things or people' and **venir chercher/prendre** 'come and pick up/fetch/collect things or people' are more or less interchangeable with **passer chercher/prendre**.

2. 'To pass' an exam is **réussir** un examen.

3. The phrase **en passant** means 'in passing'.

4. The phrase **ça passe** doubles for 'that will do' 'that's all right' 'that's satisfactory/adequate'.

5. **Passer** is also the verb used when mislaying (or losing sight of) something or someone, for example:
   - Je ne sais pas où sont passées mes clés. I don't know where my keys have got to.
   - Où étais-tu donc passé? Where on earth had you got to?

# To stay

## Rester

Ce soir je *reste* chez moi. Tonight I *am staying in* (at home).

Est-ce que vous pouvez *rester* jusqu'à midi? Can you *stay* until mid-day?

Nous voudrions *rester* trois jours. We would like *to stay* three days.

Qui compte *rester* avec moi? Who intends *to stay* with me?

Ils n'y *resteront* qu'une semaine. They *will* only *stay* there one week.

Elle *était restée* trop longtemps au soleil. She *had stayed* too long in the sun.

Leur chien adore *rester* sous la table toute la journée. Their dog loves *staying* under the table the whole day.

Il n'*est* pas *resté* dans sa chambre comme on le lui avait demandé. He *did*n't *stay* in his bedroom as we had asked him to.

Elle a préféré *rester* à l'hôtel. She chose *to stay*/to stop at the hotel.

Je regrette, vous ne pouvez pas *rester* ici. I am sorry, you cannot *stay* here.

- *Rester* means *to stay* as in 'to remain'/'to stop'/'to stay put' somewhere, that is, the opposite of 'to go' or of 'to leave'.

## To stay in a hotel

Nous *étions* dans un tout petit hôtel. We *stayed* in a very small hotel.

*Irez*-vous à l'hôtel ou chez vos amis? Will you stay in a hotel or with your friends?

Elles *ont passé* trois semaines en Suisse dans un magnifique hôtel. They *stayed* three weeks in a magnificent hotel in Switzerland.

Alors, vous *descendez* toujours à l'hôtel quand vous allez à Nantes? So, do you always *stay* in a hotel when you go to Nantes?

- *Être/aller/descendre*, 'to be', 'to go', 'to go down' *à l'hôtel*, or *passer+time* 'to spend + time' *dans un/à l'hôtel* can be used to translate *to stay in a hotel*.

## To stay in a house/flat/caravan

Ils *sont* dans un appartement pour cinq personnes. They *are staying* in a flat for five people.

Nous allons *passer* tout août dans notre caravane. We are going *to stay* in our caravan for the whole of August.

Elle *a loué* une maison près de la plage. She *stayed* in a house near the beach.

On *prendra* une villa pour dix jours. We *shall stay* in a villa for ten days.

- Again *être*, *passer* + *time*, or *louer* 'to rent' and *prendre* 'to take' can translate *to stay in a house, a flat a caravan*.

## To stay at other places

La semaine prochaine nous *serons* chez eux. We *shall be staying* with them next week.

Vous *serez/allez* dans quel camping? You *will be staying* at which campsite?

Vanessa *a passé* la nuit chez sa tante. Vanessa *stayed* the night at her aunt's.

Il veut *aller* chez son frère en Amérique. He wants *to stay* at his brother's in America.

J'espère que vous pourrez *venir chez* nous pour Pâques. I hope that you will be able to come and *stay* at Easter.

- Once again the choice, to translate *to stay* when it particularly refers to the type of accommodation is *être*, *passer* + *time*, *aller* or *venir chez*.

## Also useful to know

1. When in English 'to stay' is used to describe a type of accommodation, although not entirely right, **rester** would also always get the message across.

2.  Like **habiter**, **loger** means 'to live' as in 'to stay' more permanently than **être/aller/venir/passer/louer** etc, for example:
    - Elle peut habiter/loger chez nous, si elle veut. She can live/stay with us, if she likes.
    - On habitait en Suisse. We used to live in Switzerland.
    - Je ne sais pas où je vais loger. I don't know where I am going to live.

3.  **Séjourner** also means 'to stay' temporarily, in a village, town, area, country (not the accommodation), for example:
    - Séjourner à la campagne vous serait fort bénéfique. Staying in the countryside would be a big advantage for you.
    - Nous avons passé Le Gois, lorsque nous séjournions en Vendée. We did go across the Gois (causeway) when we were staying in Vendée.

# S'agir de = être/falloir

## S'agir de + noun

Qu'est-ce que c'est une omelette norvégienne? *Il s'agit d'*un dessert composé de glace et de meringue=C'est un dessert composé de glace et de meringue. What is a Norwegian omelette? *It is* a sweet made with ice-cream and meringue.

Je vais vous montrer des pièces anciennes, *il s'agit de* pièces grecques=Ce sont des pièces grecques. I am going to show you some very old coins, *they are* Greek coins.

Nous pourrions lui prêter cet argent puisqu'il ne *s'agit* pas *d'*une somme importante=Ce n'est pas une somme importante. We could lend him/her the money, as *it is* not a great amount.

Lorsqu'il était petit il jouait toujours avec le même 'jouet'. *Il s'agissait d'*une vieille boîte en carton qu'il tirait avec une ficelle=C'était une vieille boîte. When he was very small, he always used to play with the same 'toy'. *It was an old cardboard box which he used to pull with a string.*

It is in fact possible to replace the impossible phrase *il s'agit de* (or other tenses, of course), with 'être'. The exact translation of *il s'agit de* is: *what it/that/this is, is.*

## S'agir de + noun (or object pronoun), s'agir de + verb

Est-ce qu'*il s'agira des* enfants/*d*'eux? *Will it be about* the children/them?

Il ne *s'agissait* pas que d'argent; It *wasn't* just *about* money/*it was*n't just *a question of* money.

Il *s'agit de* respect. *It's about* respect/*it's a question of* respect.

Dans ce film, *il s'agit de* trois frères allemands qui se détestent. This film *is about* three German brothers who hate one another.

Il ne *s'agissait* pas *de* lui. *It was*n't *about* him.

Il a dit qu'*il ne s'était* jamais *agi de* ça. He said that *it had* never *been about* that.

*De* quoi *s'agit-il*? What *is it about*?

Quand *il s'agit d*'aider à la maison, c'est toujours moi. When *it's about* helping in the house/when it's a matter of helping in the house, it's always me.

A partir de demain *il s'agira d*'attendre patiemment. From tomorrow *it will be a matter of* waiting patiently.

- *S'agir de* can be translated with *to be about, to be a matter of* or *to be a question of.*

## S'agir de + verb – part 2

Il *s'agit de* répondre tout de suite=Il faut répondre tout de suite. *We/they must* reply straight away.

Que *s'agit-il de* faire?=Qu'est-ce qu'il faut faire? What *must we* do?

Il *s'agit* de montrer une pièce d'identité=Il faut montrer une pièce d'identité. *You have to* show proof of identity.

*Il* ne *s'agit* plus *de* plaisanter=Il ne faut plus plaisanter. *You must* not joke anymore.

*Il s'agit de* vous adresser à la mairie=Il faut vous adresser à la mairie. *You have to* go to the town hall for information.

*Il s'agira de* lui demander = Il faudra lui demander. *We shall have to* ask him/her.

*Il s'agissait de* regarder dans la voiture = Il fallait regarder dans la voiture. *You should have* looked in the car.

Pour appeler une ambulance *il s'agit de* composer ce numéro vert = Pour appeler une ambulance il faut composer ce numéro vert. In order to call an ambulance *you have to* dial this freephone number.

*Il s'agirait de* savoir ce que tu veux = Il faut savoir ce que tu veux. *You/we must* know what you want.

- The exact translation of *s'agir de* + *verb* could be *what you have to do/what you must do, is,* and can convey more stress than 'il faut' (must/to have to/to be necessary).

## Also useful to know

1.  The conditional form of this phrase, that is **il s'agirait de** + noun, can also mean 'it/they would appear to be', for example:

    - On vient de trouver un sac en cuir noir, et il s'agirait de mon sac. They have just found a black leather bag, and it would appear to be my bag.

    - Il s'agirait d'une erreur. It would appear to be a mistake.

2.  **Il ne s'agit pas de ça** can mean 'that's not the point.'

# Helping you learn

## Progress questions

**1** Looking at English side only, translate some examples in this chapter and check your answers.

**2** Write down explanations for when to use 's'agir (de)' and check your answers.

## Discussion point

With regard to 'on', do you agree that one never questions oddity in one's mother tongue?

## Practical assignment

When reading or listening, try changing 'on' with 'nous' and vice versa, or try to replace 's'agir (de)' with 'être' or 'falloir'.

## Study tip

Read something in French every day.

# Mastering Some Difficult Structures

**One-minute overview**

Some key structures can be difficult to master. When something or someone has been physically *missed*, the key structure is the same as the English one, but, if talking about missing something or someone in an abstract way, then what or who is missed is the subject of the verb *manquer*. *Plaire à* doubles for *aimer* but what or who is liked/loved has to be the subject of the verb. This makes for a key structure which requires a lot of getting used to. Dimanche *dernier* and *le dernier* dimanche, can be completely different dates. This chapter will show you:

- step-by-step key structures which are different from English ones
- word order differences
- a short cut to speed and perfect your fluency in French

## Manquer: *to miss*

### Manquer something, manquer someone

Malheureusement, hier j'*ai manqué* le dernier car.
> Unfortunately I *missed* the last coach yesterday.

Il *manquera* à la soirée vendredi car il doit emmener sa
femme à l'hôpital. He *will miss* the dinner and dance
on Friday because he has to take his wife to hospital.

On va encore *manquer* l'émission. We're going *to miss* the
programme again.

Je suis vraiment désolé/navré d'avoir à *manquer* votre dîner
le vingt. I really am sorry that I have *to miss* your
dinner on the twentieth.

T'aurais pas pu *manquer* ce trou sur la chaussée, enfin!
Really, couldn't you *have missed* that hole in the road!

*Manqué!* Décidément tu es nul au tir! *Missed!* Honestly
you're hopeless at shooting!

Qui *a manqué* la réunion? Who *missed* the meeting?

Qu'est-ce que *j'ai manqué?* What *did* I *miss?*

Voilà deux semaines qu'elle *manque* l'école. She *has been
missing* school for two weeks.

Vous venez de *manquer* Mireille. You have just *missed*
Mireille.

Dépêchez-vous, vous allez les *manquer!* Hurry up you are
going *to miss* them!

Ils se sont *manqués* de peu. They only just *missed* each
other.

## Things or people + manquer

Au moins cinq cartes *manquent* à ce jeu. At least five cards
in this game *are missing.*

Ce n'est que lorsque nous avons fini le puzzle que nous
nous sommes aperçus que deux pièces *manquaient.* It's
only once we finished the puzzle that we discovered
that two pieces *were missing.*

Qu'est-ce qui *manque?* What *is missing?*

Savez-vous pourquoi Renée *manque* aujourd'hui? Do you
know why Renée *is missing* today?

Qui manque? Who is missing?

* This is the key structure used when *manquer* means *to be
missing*, as in 'to be absent', not here, but should be.

## Il (impersonal) + manquer + something/someone

*Il manque* beaucoup de dents à ce peigne = Beaucoup de
dents manquent à ce peigne. A lot of teeth *are missing*
on this comb.

*Il manque* le sel sur la table = Le sel manque sur la table.
The salt *is missing* on the table/There is no salt on the
table.

*Il manquait* mon passeport dans mon sac quand on l'a
retrouvé = Mon passeport manquait dans mon sac
quand on l'a retrouvé. My passport *was missing* in my
handbag when it was found.

*Il manquera* Martin demain = Martin manquera demain.
Martin *will be missing* tomorrow.

*Il ne manque* que ma mère = Seulement ma mère manque.
Only my mother *is missing*.

- This is another key structure, to say exactly the same thing as
with the previous key structure.

## Il (impersonal) + manquer + something + someone

*Il manque* encore cinquante francs à Nicole. Nicole has got
fifty francs *missing* still (is still fifty francs short).

Elle a dit qu'*il* lui *manquait* un des ses livres. She said that
one of her books *was missing*.

*Il manque* deux valises à ce couple anglais. This English
couple have two suitcases *missing* (they are two suitcases
short).

*Il* vous *manque* un bouton. You have got one button
*missing*.

- With this key structure someone has something *missing*.

## Something/someone + manquer (à) + someone

La France leur *manque* énormément. They *miss* France
dreadfully.

La neige *manque* à mon ami en Australie. My friend in
Australia *misses* the snow.

Qu'est-ce qui vous *manque* le plus quand vous êtes en
Angleterre? What do you *miss* the most when you are
in England?

Le climat nous *manque*. We *miss* the weather.

Est-ce que je vous *ai manqué*? Did you *miss* me?

Je savais bien que ses enfants lui *manqueraient*. I knew that
he/she *would miss* his/her children.

Tu nous *manques*. We *miss* you.

Notre chien *manquera* à notre fils. Our son *will miss* our
dog.

- This structure is used when *to miss* means 'to long for' 'to
yearn for' things or people. This structure takes time to get
used to because it is what, or who is being missed which is the
subject of *manquer*. So, the literal translation is: something,
or someone is lacking to someone.

## Subject + manquer de + nouns

On va *manquer de* temps. We are going *to be short of* time.

Je pense qu'il *a* toujours *manqué de* classe. In my opinion
he *has* always *lacked* class.

A notre club international, on *manque de* jeunes hommes.
We *are short of* young men in our international club.

Vous *avez manqué de* tact hier, vous savez. You *lacked* tact
yesterday, you know.

Ils ne *manqueront* jamais *d'*argent. They *will* never *be short
of* money.

Cet hôtel *manque d'*ambiance. This hotel *lacks* atmosphere.

Elle ne *manque de* rien. She *is* not *short of* anything/she
doesn't want for anything.

- *Manquer* in this structure means *to be short of,* to lack
something.

## Also useful to know

1. **Se manquer,** also means 'to have a failed suicide
   attempt'.

2. The expressions **il ne manque/manquait/manquerait
   plus que ça** mean 'that is/was/would be the last straw'.

3. The phrase **à la manque** means 'second rate'.

# Plaire (à) = *aimer*

## to like, to love

Chrystelle aime le professeur d'anglais = Le professeur
d'anglais *plaît à* Chrystelle. Chrystelle *likes* the English
teacher.

J'aime la Belgique = La Belgique me *plaît*. I *like* Belgium.

On n'a jamais aimé le patinage = Le patinage ne nous *a*
jamais *plu*. We *have* never *liked* ice-skating.

J'espère que vous aimerez ce film = J'espère que ce film vous
*plaira*. I hope that you *will like* this film.

Il n'a pas aimé ça = Ça ne lui *a* pas *plu*. He *did*n't *like* that.

Elles aiment le rouge = Le rouge leur *plaît*. They *like* red.

Je sais qu'il l'aime beaucoup = Je sais qu'elle/il lui *plaît*
beaucoup. I know he *likes* him/her a lot.

Qu'est-ce qu'elle a le plus aimé? = Qu'est-ce qui lui *a* le plus
*plu*? What *did* she *like* best?

Tu aimes ce chanteur? = Ce chanteur te *plaît*? Do you *like*
this singer?

J'aimerais aller au cinéma = Aller au cinéma me *plairait*. I
*would like* to go to the cinema.

On a beaucoup aimé Biarritz = Biarritz nous *a* beaucoup *plu*.
We *liked* Biarritz a lot.

Elle n'aime pas la cuisine indienne = La cuisine indienne ne
lui *plaît* pas. She doesn't *like* Indian cooking.

- *Plaire* and 'aimer' are interchangeable. More often than not,
  in everyday conversation the French seem to use *plaire*. The
  literal translation with a *plaire* key structure takes a lot of
  getting used to, because it is what, or who people like or love
  which is the subject of the verb 'to please'.

## Also useful to know

**Déplaire** (à) is the opposite of **plaire** (à) and follow the
same pattern, for example:

1. Je n'aime pas cette ville = Cette ville me déplaît. I don't
   like this town.

2. Elle n'aime pas la musique classique = La musique classique lui déplaît. She doesn't like classical music.

# Prochain: *next*

## prochain + nouns

Le *prochain car* est à huit heures, je crois. The *next coach* is at eight, I believe.

Ma *prochaine voiture* sera italienne. My *next car* will be Italian.

J'expliquerai tout dans ma *prochaine lettre*. I shall explain everything in my *next letter*.

Est-ce que le *prochain village* est loin d'ici? Is the *next village* far from here?

Avez-vous décidé quel sera le titre de votre *prochain livre*? Have you decided what the title of your *next book* will be?

Je voudrais descendre au *prochain arrêt*. I would like to get out at the *next stop*.

J'expliquerai tout la *prochaine fois*. I'll explain everything *next time*.

- *Prochain* is one of the less known adjectives which is placed before nouns.

## Prochain + when

J'espère qu'il neigera le *prochain Noël* que je passerai ici. I hope that *the next Christmas* I spend here, it snows.

Le *prochain dimanche* que vous viendrez, nous ferons une excursion en bateau. *The next weekend* you come, we'll have a boat trip.

Il nous apprendra à jouer à la belote pendant le *prochain week-end* que nous passerons ensemble. He will teach us how to play belote *the next weekend* we spend together.

On repeindra le garage le *prochain samedi* qu'il ne pleut pas, hein? *The next Saturday* it doesn't rain, we'll paint the garage, shall we?

- As in English, saying *the next* + *when* usually means that a date is unknown, to be decided.

## When + prochain

Venez *dimanche prochain*. Come *next Sunday*.

Ils ont enfin décidé de venir *l'année prochaine*. They've finally decided to come *next year*.

Mireille commence *lundi prochain*. Mireille starts *next Monday*.

On va en Amérique le *mois prochain*. We're going to America *next month*.

J'irai l'*été prochain*. I shall go *next summer*.

Elle viendra sans doute la *semaine prochaine*. She will probably come *next week*.

Que faites-vous le *week-end prochain*? What are you doing *next weekend*?

- In this key structure the word order is the opposite, *next* comes after the noun it refers to, and a specific time or date (day, week, month or year) has been mentioned.

## Also useful to know

1. 'The next day' is **le lendemain.**

2. The parting pleasantry **à la prochaine** is the equivalent of the vague 'see you' or 'see you later' and is short for **à la prochaine fois,** 'until the next time (we meet)'.

### Helping you learn

**Progress questions**

1 Looking at English side only, translate some examples and check your answers.

2 Write down explanations for word order differences and check your answers.

### Discussion point

Do you ever question word order in your language?

### Practical assignment

Never miss an oportunity to visit a French speaking country.

### Study tip

Think in French every day.

# Other Useful Adverbs

Several adverbs which are in constant use in daily life are 'false friends', i.e. the words look and sound much like English ones, but they mean something else, for example the French *actuellement* does not mean *actually* but *at present* or *now*, *effectivement* actually means *indeed*, and *evidently* is not *évidemment*, but *manifestement* or *visiblement.* This chapter will show you:

- the list of the main pitfalls
- the actual translations of the main 'false friends'
- if useful, the French equivalents for adverbs in question
- how to avoid misunderstandings
- a short cut to speed and perfect your fluency in French

## Useful adverbs

### Actuellement

Ils sont *actuellement* au Canada. They are in Canada *at the moment.*

*Actuellement* il y a très peu de travail. There is very little work *at present.*

*Actuellement* ce n'est pas la mode. It is not the fashion *nowadays.*

Où habitez-vous *actuellement*? Where do you live *at the moment*?

*Actuellement* les enfants ont trop d'argent. Children have too much money *in this day and age.*

- *Actuellement* means *now, nowadays, at present, at the moment, in this day and age.*

*Actually*, he is leaving on the second of January. Il part le deux janvier, *en fait/à vrai dire.*

She didn't understand *actually*. *En fait/à vrai dire* elle n'a
pas compris.
There was nothing left *actually*. Il n'y avait plus rien, *en fait/
à vrai dire.*
It would be better, *actually*. Ce serait mieux, *en fait/à vrai
dire.*

- To translate *actually* use *en fait,*or *à vrai dire.*

She *actually* said that? A-t-elle *vraiment* dit ça?
I *actually* want to drive tomorrow. Je veux *vraiment*
conduire demain.
We *actually* believe them. On les croit *vraiment.*
I can *actually* do that. Je peux *vraiment* faire ça.

- However, when *actually* could be replaced by *really* then
*vraiment* is used.

## Carrément

Je vais lui dire *carrément* que ça ne me plaît pas du tout. I
am going to tell him/her *bluntly/straight* that I don't like
that at all.
Nous refuserions *carrément*. We would *bluntly* refuse.
Ils sont *carrément* allés voir le directeur. They went *straight*
to the manager.

- *Carrément* means *bluntly* or *straight,* that is, without hesita-
tion.

## Certainement

On leur donnera *certainement* un choix. They will *most
probably* give them a choice.
Elise arrivera *certainement* avant vous. Elise will *most
probably* arrive before you do.
Il a *certainement* tout compris. He *most probably* understood
everything.
Elle connaît *certainement* Stéphanie. She *most probably*
knows Stéphanie.

- *Certainement* very often means *most probably*.

- As in English, it can also mean *certainly,* as in *of course,* especially when just on its own.

## Effectivement

Ils s'étaient *effectivement*/en effet trompés. They had *indeed* made a mistake.

Il y a *effectivement*/en effet beaucoup de restaurants chinois par ici. There are *indeed* many Chinese restaurants near here.

J'ai *effectivement*/en effet terminé. *Indeed,* I have finished.

Ils étaient *effectivement*/en effet tous là. They were *indeed* all there.

On a *effectivement* décidé de déménager. We have *indeed* decided to move house.

- *Effectivement* means *indeed,* as does *en effet.*

- To translate *effectively* as in *efficiently,* use *efficacement.*

## En principe

*En principe,* nous nous levons à sept heures. *Usually* we get up at seven.

*En principe* ils arrivent à peu près maintenant. They *normally* arrive about now.

*En principe* on va les voir le vendredi. We *usually* visit them on Fridays.

Ils mangent à la cantine, *en principe*. They eat at school, *usually*.

Je vais chez le coiffeur une fois par semaine, *en principe*. I go to the hairdresser once a week, *usually/as a rule*.

- *En principe* mean *as a rule, usually, generally,* or *normally.*

- *Normalement* could also replace *en principe* in the examples above.

*All being well,* he will start tomorrow. *Normalement* il commence demain.

We should finish by next week, *all being well*. On devrait terminer d'ici la semaine prochaine, *normalement*.

I'll see both of you on Saturday, *all being well*. Je vous verrai tous les deux samedi, *normalement*.

- However, *normalement* can also mean *all being well*.

I don't read this newspaper *on principle*. Je ne lis pas ce journal *par principe*.

We are striking *on principle*. On fait la grève *par principe*.

Valérie says that she is a vegetarian *on principle*.Valérie dit qu'elle est végétarienne *par principe*.

- *On principle* is *par principe*.

## Evidemment

On a *évidemment* tout dépensé. *Of course* we spent everything.

*Evidemment* je t'emmènerai en voiture! *Naturally* I will give you a lift!

Après ça il l'a *évidemment* quittée. After that, *obviously*, he left her.

Il est venu, *évidemment*. He came, *of course*.

- *Evidemment* means *naturally, of course, obviously*.

- Another way of saying *naturally, of course* or *obviously* is *bien sûr*.

He will want to go with him/her, that's *obvious*/inevitable. Il voudra *forcément* l'accompagner.

People *do not necessarily* want to eat out whilst they are on holiday. Les gens ne veulent *pas forcément* manger au restaurant lorsqu'ils sont en vacances.

- *Forcément* can be one more way to translate *obviously*, perhaps more as in *inevitably*. However this adverb is very often used in the negative, when, along with *pas nécessairement*, it means *not necessarily*.

- *Forcibly* is *de/par la force*.

She was *evidently/obviously/visibly* cross. Elle était *de toute évidence/manifestement/visiblement* en colère.

They were *evidently/obviously/clearly* asleep. *Il est évident qu'/ manifestement/visiblement* ils dormaient.

This animal is *evidently/obviously/visibly* in pain. *Il est évident que/manifestement/visiblement*, cet animal souffre.

- *Evidently* as in *obviously*, can be translated with *de toute évidence*, *il est évident que*, *manifestement* or *visiblement*.

## Justement

J'y avais *justement* pensé. *Funnily enough/as a matter of fact*, I had thought about it.

*Justement*, elle l'a vue hier. *Funnily enough/as a matter of fact* she saw her yesterday.

Ils viennent *justement* de téléphoner. *Funnily enough/as a matter of fact*, they have just phoned

J'allais *justement* le faire. I was just about to do it, *funnily enough, as a matter of fact*.

- *Justement* can be used to translate *as a matter of fact* or *funnily enough*.

- On its own, *justement* can translate the exclamation *exactly!* or *precisely!*

As you *rightly/justly* said. Comme vous avez dit *justement/ avec justesse*.

The case was *justly* dealt with. Cette affaire a été traitée *justement/avec justesse*.

- *Justly* can also be translated with *justement*, or *avec justesse*.

## Sûrement

Q. Vous allez fêter votre anniversaire de mariage chez vous? A. *Sûrement!*

Q. Are you going to celebrate your wedding anniversary at home? A. *Of course!/naturally!*

Q. Il pourra les emmener chez le dentiste samedi? A.
*Sûrement!*

Q. Will he be able to take them to the dentist's on
Saturday? A. *Of course!/naturally* (he will)!

- When used as an exclamation, on its own, *sûrement* is an
alternative for *évidemment* and means *of course, naturally* or
*obviously.*

Ils fêteront *sûrement* leur anniversaire de mariage chez eux.
They will *most probably* celebrate their wedding
anniversary at home.

Elle les emmènera *sûrement* au cinéma. She will *most
probably* take them to the cinema.

Vous la verrez *sûrement* cet après-midi.You will *most
probably* see her/ you are bound to see her this
afternoon..

Elle va *sûrement* pleurer. She will *most probably* cry.

- However, when *sûrement* is part of a sentence, it can double
for *certainement* and means once again, *most probably,* or *to
be bound to.*

## Helping you learn

### Progress question

**1** Looking at French side only, translate examples in this
chapter and check your answer.

### Discussion points

**1** Discuss the difficulties of learning the language as a result
of 'false friends' with francophone friends.

**2** Discuss and ponder on possible misunderstandings arising
from using a 'false friend' wrongly.

**3** Share any such experiences.

## Practical assignment

When listening to some French (actual conversations, study cassettes, radio or television) note use of these adverbs.

## Study tips

1. Do use your French every day.

1. Never miss an opportunity to visit a French-speaking country – and especially to stay with a French family.

2. Reciprocate hospitality.

# Useful Phrases and Expressions

Literal translations are more often than not worth a try, but in the case of a handful of phrases, for example *sans doute,* it could lead to unpleasant misunderstandings and consequences, as it only means *probably,* not *without (a) doubt.* Again, the last thing you want to do when wishing to congratulate someone for their efforts is the literal translation of *well done,* as you would in fact make a rude remark. This chapter will show you:

■ the literal translations of these few phrases
■ the equivalent in French for the English phrases
■ how misunderstandings and upsets could arise
■ when to use two unclear everyday parting plaisantries
■ a short cut to speed and perfect your fluency in French

## In general conversation

### Bien fait

Although the literal translation of this phrase is *well done,* this is the French exclamation equivalent to *good,* said spitefully in England to show pleasure when something awful has happened to someone (you obviously do not like).

When wishing to encourage or congratulate someone's efforts or results, for example when a child is trying to learn to swim, or when someone has passed an exam, to say *well done* the French say *bravo!*

### Also useful to know

**Bien faire** something, however, is indeed 'to do something well'. It can also mean 'to do the right thing':

–   Il a bien fait son lit ce matin. He made a good job
    of his bed this morning.
–   Elle a bien fait de tout me dire. She did the right
    thing telling me everything.
–   Vous avez sûrement bien fait. You most probably
    did the right thing.

## C'est pas possible (ce n'est pas possible)

Il a encore la grippe? *C'est pas possible.* He has got the flu
    again? *I don't believe it!*
*C'est pas possible,* vous avez perdu le billet? *I don't believe
    this,* you have lost the ticket?
Elle a fait ça? *C'est pas possible!* She did that? *Surely not!*
Vous avez été licencié? *C'est pas possible!* You have been
    made redundant, *I don't believe it* !

- *C'est pas possible* is the French *for I don't believe it/this*! or
  *surely not*! The phrases which express great surprise,
  annoyment or upset at some news, information or situations.

## Sans doute

Il s'agit *sans doute* d'une erreur. It is *probably* a mistake.
Stéphanie a dit qu'elle viendra *sans doute* mercredi soir.
    Stephanie said that she will *probably* come wednesday
    evening.
Elle le sait *sans doute.* She *probably* knows.
Ils savent *sans doute* conduire. They *probably* can drive.
Vous comprenez *sans doute.* You *probably* understand.
Ils sont *sans doute* en vacances, actuellement. They're
    *probably* on holiday, at the moment.
C'est *sans doute* elle qui a payé. She *probably* paid.
C'est *sans doute* la meilleure solution. It's *probably* the best
    solution.
Il y est *sans doute* allé. He *probably* went (there).

- Despite its literal translation, which is 'without doubt', *sans
  doute* only means *no doubt, doubtless* or *probably.*

## Also useful to know

1.  'Without (a) doubt' is **sans aucun doute, sans nul doute** or **incontestablement**, for example:

    – C'est sans aucun doute son meilleur ami. He is without a doubt his/her best friend.
    – C'est sans aucun doute leur faute. It is their fault, without doubt.
    – Ils viendront le mois prochain, sans aucun doute. They will come next month without a doubt.

2.  Confusingly, **s'en douter** or **se douter de quelque chose** both mean 'to suspect', 'to guess' 'to gather' something, for example:

    – Il s'en doute depuis longtemps. He has suspected something for a long time.
    – Vous vous en doutiez, n'est-ce pas? You guessed, didn't you?
    – Je m'en suis douté. I gathered that.

# Partings

French people like to part on a wish. These are easy to understand except for two, which can puzzle people for some time.

## Bon courage

*Bon courage,* is the equivalent of *I'll think about you/don't lose heart/be brave/you'll be alright/take care,* obviously said to people who are going through a difficult period, or are about to face something unpleasant (problems, doctor, exam, etc). In other words, it is the appropriate parting wish for people who need moral support. *Bon courage* can also double for 'bonne chance', that is, *good luck.*

## bonne continuation

The literal translation of *bonne continuation* is obviously *good continuation* (!), as in, *may your present happy/successful life continue.* Therefore the nearest equivalent in English could be *all the best*, or *take care* particularly when you don't know when, or if, you will see the person again.

## Helping you learn

### Progress questions

1. What does *bien fait* mean? Check your answer.

2. What is the French for *well done?* Check your answer.

3. Do the same for other phrases in this chapter.

### Discussion points

1. Literal translations are usually worth a try. They usually work, except for the phrases in this chapter.

2. Discuss and ponder on possible misunderstandings arising from using the literal translations of phrases in this chapter.

3. Share any such experiences.

### Practical assignment

When reading or listening, try spotting uses of phrases in this chapter.

### Study tips

1. Do try to use all the French you know every day.

2. Never miss an oportunity to visit a French speaking country, and make the most of complete submersion.

# Choices

Having too much choice to translate English can also be confusing, and a blow to confidence. Just as some things can be said slightly differently in English, such as *you're welcome, don't mention it, not at all* and more, the same applies to French, in this *case je vous en prie, de rien, it n'y a pas de quoi*. Conversely, some English words or key structures have interchangeable possibilities in French. For *retired* there is *retraité(e), en retraite* or *à la retraite*, and *il faut rester, il faut que vous restiez,* or *vous devez rester* all mean *you must stay.* This chapter will show you:

■ that there can be a number of ways to say the same thing in both languages
■ that there are sometimes several possibilities to translate just one English word, phrase or key structure
■ some interchangeable words or phrases used with the same example deliberately, for conviction purposes
■ a short cut to speed and perfect your fluency in French

## A good choice

### Thank you
Merci. Thanks, thank you.
Je vous remercie. I thank you.
Merci bien. Thanks a lot, many thanks.
Merci beaucoup. Thank you very much.
Merci mille fois. Thank you very very much, thank you so much, thank you ever so much.

### Also useful to know
When offered something to drink or to eat, replying just 'thank you' in England means 'yes please'. In France, in similar circumstances, just answering **merci** means the opposite: 'no thank you' (it is obviously also perfectly safe to say **non merci**).

## Don't mention it/you're welcome/my pleasure/any time/not at all

Je vous en prie, can be the most formal and polite.

De rien is not at all, (there is nothing to thank me for), more informal phrase than 'je vous en prie'.

A votre service, which means glad to be of service, all part of the service (that's what I am here for) will be mainly used by people who are getting paid for whatever they are being thanked for.

C'est moi, means it's for me to thank you, a more informal way of saying 'à votre service'.

Avec plaisir, my pleasure, is often used when being thanked for favours.

Il n'y a pas de quoi, again, there is nothing to thank me for, is the most informal of all and could be used to show familiarity.

## OK

- When ordering drinks or food, feedback may be one of the following:

Oui (often more than once), oui oui oui, and usually followed by monsieur/madame.

Tout de suite, a big favourite, can mean immediately, straight away, coming up, thus showing eagerness to serve and please the customer.

Entendu, which surprisingly, literally means 'heard', and which is perhaps the English equivalent of 'I've got that'.

D'accord, is alright.

OK.

Bon, bien/très bien, are the same as very well.

Parfait, is like saying fine.

## Finalising arrangements

- At the end of making arrangements, all except 'tout de suite' in the list above could be used again, plus one of the following:

C'est ça. That's it.
Voilà. There we/you are.
Ça va. That's alright.
C'est convenu (comme ça). It's all arranged/agreed.

- As a reply, when asking permission to do something:

    Oui, oui oui oui,
    Ok,
    Ça va, and
    D'accord, again are suitable, as well as
    Bien sûr/bien entendu. Of course.
    Il n'y a pas de problème. No problem.
    Je vous en prie. Please do/feel free.

- Finally, when checking that formalities are in order, particularly when offering an alternative to what is requested, all the possible answers in the above list are suitable except for 'je vous en prie' plus:

    ça marche, or
    ça passe, which both mean that will do.

## Instructions/requests/orders/suggestions

Tournez/vous tournez/vous allez tourner à droite. Turn/you turn/you are going to turn right.
Montrez/vous montrez/vous allez montrer votre passeport. Show/you show/you are going to show your passport.
Attendez/vous attendez/vous allez attendre cinq minutes. Wait/you wait/vous are going to wait five minutes.
Parlez/vous parlez/vous allez parler plus fort. Speak/you speak/you are going to speak louder.
Restez /vous restez/vous allez rester ici. Stay/you stay/ you are going to stay here.

- To give instructions and orders, or to make requests, it is possible to use, *the imperative tense, the present tense, or, the immediate future* (present of 'aller'+infinitive).

Vous devez/Il faut/Il vous faut tourner à droite/Il faut que vous tourniez à droite. You have to turn right.

Vous devez/Il faut/Il vous faut /Il faut que vous montriez votre passeport. You need to show your passport.

Vous devez/Il faut/Il vous faut attendre /Il faut que vous attendiez cinq minutes. You must wait five minutes.

Vous devez/Il faut/Il vous faut parler plus fort /Il faut que vous parliez plus fort. You need to speak louder.

Vous devez/Il faut/Il vous faut rester ici /Il faut que vous restiez ici. You have to stay here.

- These are three more key structures which could be used to give orders, instructions or suggestions, respectively *devoir*, or, *il faut + infinitive*, or, *il faut que + subjunctive tense.*

Vous pouvez tourner à droite. You can turn right.

Vous pouvez montrer votre passeport? Can you show your passport?

Vous pouvez parler plus fort? Can you speak louder?

Vous pouvez attendre cinq minutes? Can you wait five minutes?

Vous pouvez rester ici? Can you stay here?

- Finally, *pouvoir* can also be used for suggestions, and can soften an order or a request, particularly if there is an choice.

# How much is it?

Quel est le prix? What is the price?

Combien? How much?
C'est combien? How much is it?

Cela/ça fait combien? How much does that come to?
Il/elle fait combien? How much does it cost?
Ils/elles font combien? How much do they cost?

Je vous dois combien? How much do I owe you?

Cela/ça coûte combien? How much does that cost?
Il/elle coûte combien? How much does it cost?
Ils/elles coûtent combien? How much do they cost?

Cela/ça vaut combien? How much does that cost?
Il/elle vaut combien? How much does it cost?
Ils/elles valent combien? How much do they cost?

## Also useful to know

1. One translation of **devoir** is 'to owe'.

2. The irregular verb **valoir** means 'to be worth' and is used as much as **être faire** or **coûter** when talking about prices and costs. **Cela/ça vaut la peine** is the useful expression 'it's worth the trouble'.

## Do it/this again

Hier, j'ai *encore (une fois)* vu Claude = J'ai vu Claude *de/à nouveau* hier = J'ai *re*vu Claude hier. I saw Claude *again* yesterday.

Je vais écrire *encore une fois* = Je vais écrire *de/à nouveau* = Je vais *re*-écrire. I am going to write *again*.

Elle le lui a *encore* dit = Elle le lui a dit *de/à nouveau* = Elle le lui a *re*dit. She has told him/her *again*.

Vous êtes tombé *encore une fois*? = vous êtes tombé *de/à nouveau* = Vous êtes *re*tombé? Did you fall *again*?

Nous voulons bien le faire *encore une fois* = Nous voulons bien le faire *de/à nouveau* = Nous voulons bien le *re*faire. We don't mind doing it again.

Elle est *encore* venue? = Elle est venue *de/à nouveau*? = Elle est *re*venue? Did she come *again*?

Sylvie a décidé de lire ce livre *encore une fois* = Sylvie a décidé de lire ce livre *de/à nouveau* = Sylvie a décidé de *re*lire ce livre. Sylvie has decided to read this book *again*.

Il a fallu ouvrir la valise *encore une fois* = Il a fallu ouvrir la valise *de/à nouveau* = Il a fallu *r*ouvrir la valise. We had to open the suitcase *again*.

- To do something *again* can be translated by the addition of *encore* (*une fois*), *de nouveau,* or [6] *nouveau.* The prefix '*re*+' ('re-'or just 'r' in front of some vowels) can be added to many verbs.

## Also useful to know

1. **A nouveau** can mean 'again', or 'once again', but differently as in afresh or anew, but is used just as much in conversation as the very similar phrase **de nouveau.**

2. In speech, it is also possible to add the prefix 're' to virtually all verbs, for example:

   - Vous avez re-mangé du poulet à midi? You had chicken again for lunch?
   - Il faut que tu reprennes du pain. You need to get some bread again.
   - Nous nous sommes re-regardés. we looked at each other again.

# Must

*Il faut* cuire ce plat au four pendant au moins deux heures. You *have to* cook this dish in the oven for at least two hours.

Pour passer la frontière, *il faut* posséder un passeport. In order to cross the border you *need to* have a passport.

*Il faut* avoir dix-huit ans. You *have to* be eighteen.

*Il* ne *faut* pas marcher sur la pelouse autour du château. You *must* not walk on the lawn around the castle.

*Il faut* remplir ce papier et l'envoyer à cette adresse avec deux photos. You *have to* fill in this form and send it to this address with two photographs.

- Il *faut* + *infinitive* is particularly used when talking about instructions, rules and regulations and can imply that there is not a choice. It is used widely to translate the English *you (as in people in general) have to/must/need to* (the literal translation is *it is necessary to*) + verb in the infinitive.

*Il faut* préparer le dîner. *I/we/you/they/people have to,*
*someone has to,* prepare the evening meal.

*Il faudrait* répondre à toutes ces lettres avant le cinq. *I/we/*
*you/they/people/someone should* reply to all these letters
before the fifth.

*Il a fallu réparer* le toit. *I/we/you/they/people/someone had* to
repair the roof.

*Il faudra* absolument leur téléphoner. *I/we/you/they/people/*
*someone will have to* phone them without fail.

*Il faut* laver la voiture régulièrement. *I/we/you/they/people*
*have to, someone has to,* wash the car regularly.

*Il faut* sortir la poubelle deux fois par semaine. *I/we/you/*
*they/people have to, someone has to,* take the dustbin out
twice a week.

*Il faut* travailler jusqu'à la retraite. *I/we/you/they/people have*
*to* work until retirement.

Qu'est-ce qu'il faut faire? What must *I/we/you/they/people*
*have to* do?

• Another very frequent use of this very key structure, il faut
+ infinitive, could also have 'reluctant' or vague subjects.
Despite its literal translation *il faut* is used a great deal in
everyday conversation.

*Il faut que j'*achète=*Il me faut* acheter=*je dois* acheter de
l'eau. *I must* buy some water.

*Il faudrait qu'elle* recommence=*Il lui faudrait*
recommencer=*Elle devrait* recommencer. *She should*
start again.

*Il faudra qu'ils* la quittent=Il *leur faudra* la quitter=Il*s*
*devront* la quitter. *They will have to* leave her.

*Il a fallu que nous* demandions=*Il nous a fallu*
demander=*Nous avons dû* demander. *We had to* ask.

*Il faut qu'elle* fasse la vaisselle=*Il lui faut* faire la
vaisselle=*Elle doit* faire la vaisselle. *She must* do the
washing up.

*Il a fallu que j'*écrive trois fois=*Il m'a fallu* écrire trois
fois=*J'ai dû* écrire trois fois. *I had to* write three times.

*Il faut que nous* signions tous les deux=*Il nous faut* signer tous les deux =*Nous devons* signer tous les deux. *We both have to* sign.

*Il faudra qu'il* parte avant eux=*Il lui faudra* partir avant eux=*Il doit partir* avant eux. *He has to* leave before them.

*Il faut que je* vous parle d'urgence=*Il me faut* vous parler d'urgence =*je dois* vous parler d'urgence. *I have/need to* talk to you urgently.

*Il faut que vous* vous décidiez=*Il vous faut* vous décider=*Vous devez* vous décider. *You must* make a decision.

*Il faut qu'on* l'emmène chez Karine=*Il nous faut* l'emmener=*On doit* l'emmener chez Karine tous les samedis. *We have to* take her to Karine's every Saturday.

*Il faudrait que vous* fassiez de la marche=*Il vous faudrait* faire de la marche=*Vous devriez* faire de la marche. *You should* take up walking.

- *Il faut que + subject + subjunctive, il + (who: indirect object) + - faut + infinitive*, and *subject + devoir + infinitive* are yet three other ways to say the same thing, *must*. With these, unlike in the preceding rule, the subject is always clear.

## Also useful to know

1. The polite phrase 'you shouldn't have' when one is receiving a present, or after favours, is **il ne fallait pas!**

2. As well as 'must' and 'to owe' (seen earlier) **devoir** also means 'to be due/to be supposed to', for example:
    - Il doit payer. He is due to pay, or, he must pay.
    - Nous devons partir dans dix minutes. We are due to leave, or, we must leave in ten minutes.
    - Il devait téléphoner hier. He was due to/supposed to phone yesterday.
    - Je dois les voir la semaine prochaine. I am due to see them next week.

# Retiring

Ils sont *retraités* tous les deux. They are both *retired.*

Vous êtes bien *retraité*? You are *retired* aren't you?

Elle est *en/à la retraite* depuis six mois seulement. She has only been *retired* six months.

Mes parents ne sont pas encore *en/à la retraite*. My parents *are* not *retired* yet.

J'attends avec impatience d'être *en/à la retraite*. I can't wait to be *retired.*

* Être *retraité(e)*, être *en retraite* and être *à la retraite,* are all three interchangeable phrases to say to be *retired.*

Elles *ont pris la/leur retraite* en 1987. They *retired* in 1987.

Je vais *prendre la/ma retraite* avant mon mari. I am going *to retire* before my husband does.

Il veut *prendre la/sa retraite*. He wants *to retire.*

Quand est-ce que vous *avez pris la/votre retraite*? When *did* you *retire*?

Malheureusement, nous ne pouvons pas *prendre la/notre retraite.* Unfortunately we cannot *retire.*

* *To retire* is *prendre la,* or, *sa retraite.*

## Also useful to know

**La retraite** is 'retirement'. **Un(e) retraité(e)** is 'a pensioner'.

**La préretraite** is 'early retirement.'

# Shopping

Je *ferai les courses/des achats/les commissions/les provisions/du shopping* avant de rentrer ce soir. I *shall do the shopping* before getting home tonight.

Il faut que *je fasse les courses/des achats/les commissions/les provisions/du shopping*. I have *some shopping to do.*

Pourriez-*vous faire les courses/des achats/les commissions/les provisions/du shopping* aujourd'hui? Could you *do the shopping* today?

Elle *a* déjà *fait les courses/des achats/les commissions/les provisions/du shopping* pour le week-end. She *has* already *done the shopping* for the weekend.

On n'aime *pas faire les courses/des achats/les commisions/les provisions/du shopping*. We don't like *shopping*.

Il faut toujours *faire* trop de *courses/d'achats/de commissions/ de provisions/de shopping* à Noël. There is always too much *shopping* to be done at Christmas time.

On *fait* toujours *nos courses/commissions/provisions, notre shopping* ensemble. We always *go shopping* together.

Où *ferez*-vous *les courses/commissions/provisions, le shopping.* Where *will* you *shop?*

- *Faire les, ses,* or *des provisions* and *faire les, ses,* or *des commissions* usually mean *to shop* when talking about food shopping, whereas *faire les, ses,* or *des courses, faire des,* or *ses achats*, and, *faire du shopping* mean to shop, to go shopping in general.

## Also useful to know

1. For food shopping people also say **faire le/son marché** (whether or not going to an actual market), **aller aux commissions** (or **au supermarché** etc. of course) or, very colloquial, **acheter le/à manger**.

2. **Aller en ville** or, **aux magasins** is another way of saying 'to go shopping.'

3. 'To go **window-shopping**' is **lécher les vitrines/faire du lèche-vitrine** or **faire les magasins**.

4. **Faire une course/une commission** also means 'to do/ run an errand', for example:
   - Tu peux me faire une course demain? Can you do an errand for me tomorrow?
   - J'ai une course à faire avant de rentrer. I have an errand to do before I go home.
   - Il avait une course à faire pour son père. He had an errand to do for his father.

5. **Faire une commision** also means 'to give a message',
   for example:
   – J'espère qu'il vous a fait ma commission hier soir. I
     hope that he did give you my message last evening.
   – Je lui ferai la commission sans faute. I will give
     him/her the message without fail.

# Only

## *Ne ... que* and *seulement*

Je *n*'ai *qu*'un enfant = J'ai *seulement* un enfant. I have *only*
   one child.

Il *n*'a emporté *que* deux pantalons = Il a *seulement* emporté
   deux pantalons. He *only* took two pairs of trousers
   (with him).

Elle *n*'a écrit *qu*'à Jacques = Elle a *seulement* écrit à Jacques.
   She *only* wrote to Jacques.

On *n*'avait vu *que* monsieur Lerois = On avait vu *seulement*
   Monsieur Lerois. We had *only* seen M. Lerois.

Ils *n*'ont *qu*'une voiture = Ils ont *seulement* une voiture. They
   *only* have one car.

Vous *ne* travaillez *que* le samedi? = Vous travaillez *seulement*
   le samedi? Do you *only* work on Saturdays?

Nous *n*'aurons *qu*'une demi-heure = Nous aurons *seulement*
   une demi-heure. We shall *only* have half an hour.

Je *n*'ai *que* cent francs = J'ai *seulement* cent francs. I *only*
   have one hundred francs.

• *Ne* (verb) *que*, and *seulement* are interchangeable. Perhaps
  *seulement* could imply regret.

# Parking

Jean-Baptiste *a garé/mis/laissé sa voiture* derrière la
   banque = Jean-Baptiste *s'est garé* derrière la banque.
   Jean-Baptiste *has parked the car* behind the bank.

Elle *garera/mettra/laissera la voiture* devant mon école = Elle
   *se garera* devant mon école. She *will park* in front of my
   school.

Ils *avaient garé/mis/laissé leur voiture* près d'ici = Ils *s'étaient garés* près d'ici. They *had parked* their car near here.

Je vais *garer/mettre/laisser la voiture* dans le parking souterrain = Je vais *me garer* dans le parking souterrain. I am going *to park* the car in the underground car park.

Nous *garions/mettions/laissions* toujours *la voiture* dans la rue Sainte = Nous *nous garions* toujours dans la rue Sainte. We always *used to park* in the Sainte Street.

Où puis-je *garer/mettre/laisser la voiture*? = Où puis-je *me garer*? Where can I *park*?

Elle ne sait plus où elle *a garé/mis/laissé la voiture* = Elle ne sait plus où elle *s'est garée*. She has forgotten where she *has parked the car*.

Il me faut *garer la voiture* = Il me faut *me garer*. I must *park the car*.

J'étais en train de *garer la voiture* quand je les ai vus = J'étais en train de *me garer* quand je les ai vus. I was in the middle of *parking the car* when I saw them.

Nous essayons de *garer la voiture* depuis plus d'une heure = Nous essayons de *nous garer* depuis plus d'une heure. We have been trying *to park the car* for more than one hour.

Quand va-t-on *garer* la voiture? = Quand va-t-on *se garer*? When are we going *to park the car*?

Finalement j'ai décidé de *garer la voiture* et de continuer à pied = Finalement j'ai décidé de *me garer* et de continuer à pied. In the end I decided *to park the car* and walk.

- *Garer la voiture* and *se garer* are interchangebale. As in English, *mettre (to put) la voiture*, and *laisser (to leave) la voiture* can also be used when the location is mentioned.

## Also useful to know

1. **Stationner** means 'to park' (+'to stop' or 'to wait') but is mainly used on public notices (stationnement interdit/unilatéral/gênant etc).

2.  **Un parking**, or, **un parc de stationnement** is 'a car park' and **une aire de stationnement** is a 'parking area' between towns.

# Tag questions

Your husband is French, *isn't he*?

Votre mari est français, *n'est-ce pas*? = Votre mari est *bien* français? = Votre mari est français, *hein*? = Votre mari est français, *non*? = Votre mari est français, *pas vrai*?

She has gone back to work, *hasn't she*?

Elle a repris le travail, *n'est-ce pas*? = Elle a *bien* repris le travail? = Elle a repris le travail, *hein*? = Elle a repris le travail, *non*? = Elle a repris le travail, *pas vrai*?

They come every Tuesday, *don't they*?

Ils viennent tous les mardis, *n'est-ce pas*? = Ils viennent *bien* tous les mardis? = Ils viennent tous les mardis, *hein*? = Ils viennent tous les mardis, *non*? = Ils viennent tous les mardis, *pas vrai*?

You arrived late *didn't you*?

Vous êtes arrivé en retard, *n'est-ce pas*? = Vous êtes *bien* arrivé en retard? = Vous êtes arrivé en retard, *hein*? = Vous êtes arrivé en retard, *non*? = Vous êtes arrivé en retard, *pas vrai*?

Richard told him/her that he would come the day after tomorrow, *didn't he*?

Richard lui a dit qu'il viendrait après demain, *n'est-ce pas*? = Richard lui a *bien* dit qu'il viendrait après-demain? = Richard lui a dit qu'il viendrait après-demain, *hein*? = Richard lui a dit qu'il viendrait après-demain, *non*? = Richard lui a dit qu'il viendrait après-demain, *pas vrai*?

*   *N'est-ce pas, bien, hein* (more a noise than a word), *non* and *pas vrai* can all turn a statement into a tag question (when wishing to double-check some information). *Hein, non* and *pas vrai* are very colloquial forms. All come at the end of the

sentence, except for *bien* which needs to be straight after the verb (or after the first part of the verb for compound tenses).

You don't eat meat, *do you?*
Vous ne mangez pas la viande, *n'est-ce pas?* = Vous ne mangez pas la viande *hein?* = Vous ne mangez pas la viande, *pas vrai?*

They don't live in France, *do they?*
Ils n'habitent pas en France, *n'est-ce pas?* = Ils n'habitent pas en France, *hein?* = Ils n'habitent pas en France, *pas vrai?*

She wasn't tired, *was she?*
Elle n'était pas fatiguée, *n'est-ce pas?* = Elle n'était pas fatiguée, *hein?* = Elle n'était pas fatiguée, *pas vrai?*

He didn't pay, *did he?*
Il n'a pas payé, *n'est-ce pas?* = Il n'a pas payé, *hein?* = Il n'a pas payé, *pas vrai?*

You have never phoned him/her, *have you?*
Vous ne lui avez jamais téléphoné, *n'est-ce pas?* = Vous ne lui avez jamais téléphoné, *hein?* = Vous ne lui avez jamais téléphoné, *pas vrai?*

Valérie will not come with us, *will she?*
Valérie ne viendra pas avec nous, *n'est-ce pas?* = Valérie ne viendra pas avec nous, *hein ?* = Valérie ne viendra pas avec nous, *pas vrai ?*

- However, the *bien* and *non* key structures cannot be used in negative questions.

## Helping you learn

### Progress questions

1. List different ways to say same thing,

2. and check your answers.

### Discussion points

**1** Sometimes there are a number of slightly different ways to say the same thing in English.

**2** The same can happen in French.

**3** Do you agree that you never question your mother tongue?

### Practical assignment

Discuss and bemoan 'unnecessary' choices with fellow students.

### Study tips

**1** Write, speak, listen and think in French.

**2** Extend and perfect your foreign language every day.

# Using the Right Pronunciation

## One-minute overview

In this chapter we will be looking at problems with pronunciation and the importance of tone of voice. There doesn't seem to be a full picture about if and when a 'liaison' has to be made. Pronunciation gets even more complicated when a handful of useful words turn out to have more than one way to pro-nounce them. This unfortunate reality includes the pronunciation of some numbers; *dix* for example, can have one of three pronunciations. *Plus* (which can mean more or the opposite, *no* more) can have one of three pronunciations: the last letter is not pronounced, it is pronounced like an 's', or it is pronounced like a 'z'. On the other hand, non-verbal communication can determine whether *je veux bien* means *I would love to* or the opposite *I couldn't care less*. This chapter will show you:

■ that liaisons are not essential for getting the message across
■ that liaisons will become automatic with practice
■ when and why to pronounce the words in question differently
■ how to pronounce them
■ the important role of non-verbal communication
■ a short cut to speed and perfect your fluency in French

## Liaisons

The final consonant of French words is usually silent. Sometimes, however, when the next word begins with a vowel or 'h', a liaison is made, that is, the last consonant of the word is pronounced. Nearly every French textbook or grammar book gives a list of rules for liaisons. Short or long lists of liaisons you must make, liaisons you may make, and liaisons you must never make can be confusing, not least because they inevitably include exceptions.

When not sure whether or not to do a liaison, the golden rule is simple: don't. The good news is that people will always understand everything that is said when the liaisons have been left out, whereas they might not, when liaisons are made when they shouldn't be!

The other equally good news is that liaisons will eventually become automatic, for the simple reason that most of the time the piece in question is easier to say with the liaisons, than without them, for example: 'on-a des-amis en-Espagne' (with liaisons) is easier to say than 'on a des amis en Espagne' (without liaisons).

# Plus: three pronunciations

- The final 's' is never pronounced whenever *plus* (part of 'ne plus') means *no more, not any more, no longer,* or *not any longer.*

Il n'y avait plus de pain. There was no more bread.
Nous n'irons plus chez Céline. We shall not go to Celine's any more.
Mes amis n'ont plus de voiture. My friends don't have a car any more.
Vous ne fumez plus? You don't smoke any more?
Ils ne travaillent plus ici. They don't work here any more.
Il ne pleuvait plus. It wasn't raining any more.
Je n'ai plus d'argent. I haven't got any more money.

- When plus means *more*, it can have one of three pronunciations. The final 's' is not pronounced whenever *plus* is directly followed by an adjective or an adverb beginning with a consonant.

Il a toujours été plus grand que son frère. He has always been taller than his brother.

Je pense que cette chaise est beaucoup plus confortable que celle-ci. I think that his chair is much more comfortable than this one.

Est-ce que c'est le pub le plus proche de l'hôtel? Is that the closest pub to the hotel?

Nous avons marché plus lentement qu'eux. We walked more slowly than they did.

Le car serait plus cher. The coach would be more expensive.

Celle-là est plus belle que celle-ci. That one is more pretty than this one.

Il est arrivé beaucoup plus tard. He arrived much later.

Je voudrais un morceau plus petit. I'd like a smaller piece.

- A liaison is made, the 's' is pronounced like a 'z', when *plus* is fol-lowed by an adjective or an adverb which begins with a vowel or an 'h' (unless the 'h' is aspirate, dictionaries show which ones are).

Elle est plus âgée que Gaëlle. She is older than Gaëlle.

On a passé la journée plus agréablement qu'hier. We had a more pleasant day than yesterday.

La petite table était devenue plus instable. The small table had become more unsteady.

On ne peut pas parler plus ouvertement que ça. You can't speak more openly than that.

Cela n'aurait pas pu être plus inattendu. It couldn't have been more unexpected.

Le film était plus intéressant que celui de la semaine dernière. The film was more interesting than last week's.

Il faudrait qu'ils soient plus humains. They should be more humane.

- The 's' is pronounced when *plus* refers to the verb (and it can mean *the most*, as well as *more*).

Il pleut plus ici. It rains more here.

Ce que nous aimons le plus, c'est le sport. What we enjoy most of all is sport.

Il travaillera plus à partir de mai. He will work more from

May onwards.

Je ne sais pas pourquoi je mange toujours plus en vacances.
I don't know why I always eat more when I am on
holiday.

Vous avez voyagé plus que nous. You have travelled more
than we have.

C'est ce qui l'a inquiété le plus. That's what worried him
most.

Avec ce nouveau travail, il lui faut conduire beaucoup plus
maintenant. He has to do a lot more driving now, with
this new job.

- The 's' may be pronounced after *plus de* + noun.

Elle a plus de chance que moi. She has more luck than me.

J'ai enfin plus de temps maintenant. At last I have more
time.

Si on avait plus d'argent, on achèterait un bateau. If we had
more money, we would buy a boat.

Voulez-vous un peu plus de pain? Would you like a bit
more bread?

Il y a plus de maisons dans cette rue que dans la mienne.
There are more houses in this street, than (there are) in
mine.

Elle aimerait avoir plus de vêtements. She would like to
have more clothes.

Ils avaient envoyé plus de lettres que d'habitude. They had
sent more letters than usual.

Il a eu plus de courage que lui. He had more courage than
him.

- The 's' is pronounced when *plus* means *plus.*

Il a dit qu'ils seront sept, plus deux chiens. He said that
there will be seven of them plus two dogs.

Vous me devez trente francs pour les timbres, plus vingt-
cinq francs pour les glaces. You owe me thirty francs
for the stamps, plus twenty-five francs for the
icecreams.

Sept plus onze égale dix-huit. Seven plus eleven equals eighteen.

## Also useful to know

1. Ni plus ni moins (no more no less): 's' is not pronounced (negative).

2. Plus ou moins (More or less): 's' pronounced like a 'z'.

3. De plus en plus (more and more): first 's' pronounced like a 'z', and second 's' may be pronounced (like an 's').

4. En plus/de plus (on top of that/ furthermore/ what is more): 's' may be pronounced.

5. Au plus/tout au plus (at the most): 's' may be pronounced.

As demonstrated, all the explanations above for the different pronunciations of *plus* are hardly helpful when it comes to set expressions.

# Tous

- The 's' is not pronounced when *tous* is followed by a noun.

Nous irions en Angleterre *tous les ans*. We would go to England *every year*.

Je connaissais *tous ses amis*. I used to know *all his/her friends*.

*Tous les cars* partent de la Grande Place. *All the coaches* go from the Grande square.

*Tous mes enfants* me manquent de plus en plus. I miss *all my children* more and more.

*Tous les matins*, Patrice l'emmène au travail. *Every morning*, Patrice takes him/her to work.

Elle a lu *tous ses livres*. She has read *all his/her books*.

*Tous les journaux* ont déjà été vendus. *All the newspapers* have already been sold.

Il vient *tous les mois*. He comes *every month*.

- When *tous* means *all of them, all of you, all of us*, the 's' is pronounced.

Est-ce qu'ils viendront *tous*? Will they *all* come?

Ces vases me plaisent *tous*. I like these vases, *all of them*.

Ils fumaient *tous*. They *all* used to smoke.

Vous voulez *tous* la choucroute? Do *all of you* want the sauerkraut?

Est-ce que vous étiez *tous* demandeurs d'emploi? Were you *all* unemployed?

Vous pouvez *tous* rester jusqu'à midi. You can *all* stay until noon.

On a parlé *tous* à la fois. We *all* talked at once.

Nous avons *tous* apprécié le weekend. We *all* enjoyed the weekend.

Nous travaillons *tous* dans le même bureau. We *all* work in the same office.

## Also useful to know

The translation for 'all of you/us/them' when everyone is female is, of course, **toutes**.

# Pronouncing numbers

## Deux and trois

- The last letter of the numbers deux or *trois* are not pronounced when the words are on their own, or when the next word begins with a consonant, as in the examples below.

Q. Combien d'enfants avez vous? A. J'en ai deux/trois.

Q. How many children do you have? A. I have two/three.


Q. Une table pour combien de personnes? A. Deux/trois.

Q. A table for how many? A. Two/three.


Q. Elle aura combien de semaines de congé par an? A. seulement deux/trois.

Q. How many weeks a year annual leave will she get? A. Only two/three.

On m'a dit qu'il habite au numéro deux/trois. I was told that he lives at number two/three.

Il y a deux/trois cars par jour pour Nice, je crois. I think that there are two/three coaches a day going to Nice.

Nous faisions de la marche deux/trois fois par semaine. We used to go walking two/three times a week.

Ils ont deux/trois voitures maintenant. They have two/three cars now.

Sacha a mangé deux/trois sandwichs au fromage. Sacha has eaten two/three cheese sandwiches.

C'est à trente-deux/trois kilomètres. It's thirty-two/three kilometres away.

- However, a liaison is made, and the 'x' and 's' are pronounced like a 'z' when the next word begins with a vowel or a mute 'h'.

Il a quarante deux/trois ans après demain. He is forty two/three (years old) the day after tomorrow.

Ils ont habité à Marseille pendant deux/trois ans. They lived in Marseilles for two/three years.

Il a deux/trois idées intéressantes. He has two/three interesting ideas.

Elle a décidé d'acheter deux/trois ananas. She decided to buy two/three pineapples.

Dans ce village il n'y avait que deux/trois hôtels. There were only two/three hotels in that village.

Le film commence à deux/trois heures. The film starts at two/three o'clock.

## Quatre

- *Quatre* has two syllables, except when the next word does not begin with a vowel or an 'h', when the last two letters of the word (re) are often swallowed completely and 'quatre' then could sound like something between 'cut' and 'cat', as it could do, in all the examples below.

Je voudrais quatre timbres pour l'Angleterre. I'd like four stamps for England.

Nous attendons sa reponse depuis quatre jours. We have
    been waiting for his/her reply for four days.

Ils ont réservé quatre chambres. They have booked four
    double bedrooms.

Elle a quatre chats et quatre chiens. She has four cats and
    four dogs.

Ce cendrier coûte soixante-quatre francs madame. This
    ashtray costs sixty-four francs.

Nous avons contacté vingt-quatre personnes. We got in
    touch with twenty-four people.

# Cinq

- The final letter of *cinq* is pronounced, but the 'q' may not be
  pronounced when the next word does not begin with a vowel
  or a mute 'h', as in all the examples below.

Elle a téléphoné il y a cinq minutes. She phoned five
    minutes ago.

J'ai emporté cinq serviettes. I took five towels (with me).

Nous aurons besoin de cinq chaises. We shall need five
    chairs.

Il veut acheter cinq bics. He wants to buy five biros.

Ça fait cinquante-cinq francs. That comes to fifty-five
    francs.

On a conduit quatre-vingt-cinq kilomètres en tout. We
    drove eighty-five kilometres altogether.

## *Six* and *dix*

- The 'x' is pronounced like an 's' when *six* or *dix* are on their
  own, or are the last word of a sentence, as in the following
  examples:

Q.  Combien de pommes voulez-vous? A. Six/dix.

Q.  How many apples would you like? A. Six/ten.

Q.  Vous vous connaissez depuis combien d'années? A. Six/
    dix.

Q.  How many years have you known each other? A. Six/
    ten.

J'en prendrai six/dix. I'll have six/ten (of them).

Nous serons six/dix. There will be six/ten of us.

Il n'en a vu que six/dix. He only saw six/ten (of them).

- However, the 'x' is pronounced like a 'z' when the next word begins with a vowel or a mute 'h', as in the examples below.

Elle a six/dix enfants. She has six/ten children.

J'y ai travaillé pendant six/dix ans. I worked there for six/ten years.

Donnez-moi six/dix oranges. Can I have six/ten oranges please.

Il est déjà six/dix heures et demie. It's already half past six/ten.

Tu pourrais me prendre six oeufs? Could you get me six eggs?

- Finally, the 'x' is not pronounced when the next word doesn't begin with a vowel or a mute 'h', as in the examples below:

J'ai envoyé six/dix cartes postales. I sent six/ten postcards.

On l'a vu il y a au moins six mois. We saw him at least six months ago.

Il m'a prêté six/dix cassettes. He has lent me six/ten cassettes.

J'ai fait six/dix tasses de thé. I've made six/ten cups of tea.

Son fils a passé son permis de conduire six/dix fois avant de le réussir. His/her son took the driving test six/ten times before passing.

Philippe est malade depuis six jours exactement. Philippe has been ill for six days exactly.

Voilà dix minutes que nous attendons. We have been waiting for ten minutes.

## Huit

- The 't' is pronounced when *eight* is on its own or the last word in a sentence, and also when the next word begins with a vowel or a mute 'h' (liaison).

Q. Combien de fois avez-vous vu ce film? A. huit.
Q. How many times have you seen this film? A. Eight.

Q. Vous voulez combien de croissants? A. Huit.
Q. How many croissants would you like? A. Eight.

On devait arriver le huit. We were due to arrive on the
    eighth.

Q. Il y a combien de personnes dans la salle d'attente? A.
    huit.
Q. How many people are there in the waiting room? A.
    Eight.

Il lui en aura donné huit. He will have given him/her eight
    (of them).
Votre numéro est bien trente, soixante trois, dix-huit? Your
    (telephone) number is thirty, sixty-three eighteen, isn't it?
On quittera Paris le vingt-huit. We shall leave Paris on the
    twenty-eighth.
J'ai apporté huit assiettes jetables pour le pique-nique. I
    have brought eight throwaway plates for the picnic.
Regarde ces huit oiseaux, ce sont huit hirondelles. Look at
    these eight birds, they are eight swallows.
Il va y avoir huit émissions sur la Provence. There are going
    to be eight programmes about Provence.
On a trouvé huit erreurs. We have found eight mistakes.
Elle a choisi ces huit images. She chose these eight pictures.
M. Faure possède huit usines. M. Faure owns eight factories.
Elle a écrit huit histoires. She has written eight stories.
Je ne voudrais que huit escargots. I'd like only eight snails.

• The 't' is not pronounced when the next word doesn't begin
  with a vowel or a mute 'h'.

Je connais huit Suisses. I know eight Swiss people.
Elle a huit paires de chaussures. She has eight pairs of shoes.
Il vous faudra huit bouteilles de vin. You will need eight
    bottles of wine.

Nous aurions acheté huit baguettes. We would have bought eight baguettes.

Ils ont huit petits-enfants maintenant. They have eight grandchildren now.

Ils aimeraient rester jusqu'au huit mai. They would like to stay until the eighth of May.

J'ai perdu huit kilos. I have lost eight kilos.

Est-il possible de réserver une table pour dix-huit personnes? Is it possible to book a table for eighteen people?

J'ai huit livres de cet auteur. I have eight books by this writer.

## Neuf

- The final 'f' of *neuf* is always pronounced, as in the following examples, but for a couple of exceptions given in the next rule.

Nous avons visité neuf petits musées. We visited nine small museums.

Neuf billets, s'il vous plaît. Nine tickets please.

Il est né le neuf novembre. He was born on the ninth of November.

J'ai écrit neuf fois. I have written nine times.

Je m'occupe de neuf enfants tous les matins. I look after nine children every morning.

Il n'y a que neuf pommes de terre. There are only nine potatoes.

On trouve neuf hôtels dans mon village. There are nine hotels in my village.

- However, the final 'f' is pronounced like a 'v' in front of 'heures' and the word 'ans'.

Nicole a rendez-vous chez le dentiste à neuf heures. Nicole has a nine o' clock dental appointment.

Mon cousin n'a que neuf ans. My cousin is only nine.

# Tone of voice

## Terrible

Sa nouvelle chanson est *terrible* hein! His/her new song is *brilliant/awful*, isn't it!

Quelle nouvelle *terrible*! What a *terrific/dreadful* piece of news!

On a vu un film *terrible*. We saw a *terrible/great* film.

C'était un acteur *terrible*. He was a *fantastic/awful* actor.

Il a eu une chance *terrible*. He had an *amazing* piece of luck.

C'est une *terrible* maladie. It's a *terrible* illness.

- In France, non-verbal communication can play a big part in speech. Tone of voice, together with facial expressions and gestures, can alter the meaning of some words or expressions. This is the case with *terrible*, which can have opposite meanings, *brilliant* or *awful*.

## Bien

*Ils veulent bien* aller à la piscine avec toi. They *would love to go*/They *don't mind* going to the swimming pool with you.

Il veut venir? *Je veux bien*. He wants to come ? *That would be brilliant/I couldn't care less*.

Elle *aime bien* ce professeur. She *loves/She doesn't mind* this teacher.

Vous parlez *bien* le français quand même. Your French *is good/is not bad*, actually.

La machine marche *bien* maintenant. The machine goes *alright*/goes *really well* now.

Nous *avons bien aimé* la pièce. We *did enjoy/quite liked* the play.

- Intonation can also change the meaning of the word bien in certain contexts. *Bien* can show enthusiasm. On the other hand, depending on tone of voice (and probably facial expression, and/or gestures) *bien* could convey non-commitment or indifference.

# Helping you learn

## Progress questions

**1** Write down explanations for different pronunciations of same words, and check your answer.

## Discussion points

**1** 'These rules may seem to be the last straw'.

**2** Do you agree that some English pronunciations must give foreigners a bad time?

**3** There is no point in trying to fight rules which help to learn a language. It's easier, and more useful, to accept them!

## Practical assignment

Say examples with *plus* when it means *more* and the 's' should be pronounced like a 'z' without making a liaison. Say them with liaisons. Which is easier to say?

## Study tips

**1** Never give up when confronted with difficulties covered in *Better French*.

**2** Don't worry when things don't fall into place straight away.

**3** Everyone goes through the same experience.

**4** The only secret is practice.

# Web Sites and Useful Addresses for Students

## One-minute overview

The internet, or world wide web, is an amazingly useful resource, giving the student nearly free and almost immediate information on any topic. Ignore this vast and valuable store of materials at your peril! The following web sites may help you. Please note that neither the author nor the publisher is responsible for content or opinions expressed on the sites listed, which are simply intended to offer starting points for students. Also, please remember that the internet is a fast-changing environment, and links may come and go. If you have some favourite sites you would like to see in future editions of this book, please write to Monique Jackman, c/o Studymates (address on back cover), or email her at the address below. You will find a free selection of useful and readymade student links at the Studymates web site. Happy surfing!

http://www.studymates.co.uk
mjackman@studymates.co.uk

Disclaimer
Neither Studymates Publishing nor the author nor any/all agents for Studymates is endorsing any of the products or services that follow. We simply provide this information for the reader. Readers are advised, where appropriate, to take suitable professional and legal advice. Studymates and the author and any/all Studymates agents cannot be held responsible for outcomes of any transactions/communications both

written, verbal and via any form of media that may take place between the reader and any of the product or service suppliers mentioned here.

# For students

*L'Alliance Française*
http://www.alliancefrancaise.fr/
The home page of the leading French cultural and language teaching organisation, which has branches worldwide.
'Chaque année, 350 000 étudiants de tous âges, de toutes nationalités et de toutes professions utilisent les services de l'Alliance Française.'

*Hachette*
http://www.hachette-livre.fr/
'Éditeur de livres répondant aux besoins d'éducation, de connaissance, de culture et de loisirs pour un large public en France et à l'étranger.'

*Ici Campus*
http://www.icicampus.com/
'Guide internet pour les étudiants: études, cours, formation, écoles et universités.'

*Librairie Online*
http://www.librairieonline.com/tg/
A French supplier of books, videos, CDs and other products online.

# Web sites about France

*Inside Paris*
http://www.inside-paris.com
'Sortir à Paris: les musées, les soirées, les restaurants et les boîtes.'

*Le Figaro*
http://www.lefigaro.fr/
Home page of the famous French newspaper.

*Le Monde*
http://www.lemonde.fr/
'Journal complet et dossiers en ligne.'

*My Paris*
http://www.myparis.com/
'Quartiers, lieux célèbres, boutiques, monuments, musées, spectacles, culture, conseils et annonces immobilières, renseignements administratifs, événements et communautés.'

*Paris Match*
http://www.parismatch.com/
The home page of the famous illustrated news magazine.

*Paris Web*
http://www.paris-web.com/
A clearly-presented portal sites to all aspects of life in Paris.

*La Sorbonne*
http://www.sorbonne.fr/
'Le bâtiment, son histoire, les établissements, services et formations, les événements et une visite.'

*www.france.com*
This is a very useful site; here is what they have to say about themselves:

*France.com is your one-stop online location for everything France! If you need it, France.com truly is "he fastest way to France'! Be sure to check our forums, featured articles, news, and hotel listings of the best hotels in France.*

It is worth a look.

*http://uk.franceguide.com/*
Very handy for planning your holidays. Obviously we picked the site relevant to Brits but if you are reading this in another country you will be able to access the site and get information relevant to your trip from the country where you are now.

*http://www.airfrance.com/*
Speaks for itself, great way to travel. If you do use them as a carrier, do make sure you flash this book around whilst on board, well we do want you to look super cool!

*http://www.meteofrance.com/FR/index.jsp*
The weather forecast and quite rightly this is in French. Well, this will not be a problem for such a sophisticated traveller and linguist as you, now will it.

*http://www.bnf.fr/*
Details about libraries etc. On the day we visited we were promised an English translation sometime in the future, c'est ne pas problem maintenant, nous parlons Francais!

*http://www.afp.com/english/home/*
Claims to be the world's oldest established news agency, you need to decide for yourself. Useful if you are on business in France, we found it very up to date on the day we visited.

*http://www.louvre.fr/louvrea.htm*
This is a delight, almost as much as the museum itself. If you are in the area, well you have been working hard and after all it would only be an hour or so and will the boss really know? Well we won't tell, go for it!

*http://www.lonelyplanet.com/destinations/europe/france/*
To be highly recommended, an excellent site and top quality products.

*http://www.franceway.com/*
We liked this site; it is a site dedicated to what France has
to offer. We particularly liked the practical information
section and they are to be commended on the help they
offer to wheelchair users and others with disabilities, here
are some useful addresses from the site.

*http://www.seafrance.com*
Speaks for itself.

*http://www.mappy.fr/*
Excellent for route mapping in France. Remember to click
on the Union Flag if you want the English version.

# Search engines

*Ecila*
http://www.ecila.fr/
A structured directory and search engine, rather like Yahoo!
in appearance.

*Search Engines of France*
http://www.searchenginecolossus.com/France.html
A very useful collection of French-based search engines and
directories quick and easy to use.

*Yahoo! France*
http://fr.yahoo.com/
An essential search engine and directory to all things French.

# Some French newsgroups

To access any of these newsgroups, just type its address as
shown below into your browser's address panel, and the
messages in that newsgroup should open up automatically.

*News:alt.france*
This is smaller discussion group, but the messages are
almost all in French.

*News:fr.rec.cuisine*
Typically contains about 1,500 messages, in French, all
about recipes and cookery ideas.

*News:fr.rec.sport.football*
For soccer enthusiasts.

*News:soc.culture.french*
This group normally contains over 1,000 messages posted by
people with a variety of different interests in French culture
and society. However, most of the messages are in English.

# Useful Addresses

## British Embassies and Consulates
*www.britishembassy.gov.uk*
**If you are in trouble, then do turn to them, that is why
they are in the country. They are at**
35 rue du faubourg
St Honore 7538  Paris Cedex 08
Tel: +33 (0)1 44 51 31 00
Fax: +33 (0)1 44 51 41 27
Opening Hours: 9h30-13h00/14h30-18h00

As well as this, there is

**Paris Consulate**
18 bis, rue d'Anjou
75008 Paris
Tel: +33 (0)1 44 51 31 02
Fax: +33 (0)1 44 51 31 27

**Bordeaux Consulate**
353, boulevard du Président Wilson
33073 Bordeaux Cedex
Tel: +33 (0)5 57 22 21 10
Fax: +33 (0)5 56 08 33 12
Opening Hours: 9h00-12h00/14h00-17h00 Monday to Friday

### Lille Consulate
11 square Dutilleul
59800 Lille
Tel: +33 (0)3 20 12 82 72
Fax: +33 (0)3 20 54 88 16
Opening Hours: 9h30-12h30/14h00-17h00 Monday to
Friday

### Lyon Consulate
24, rue Childebert
69002 Lyon
Tel: +33 (0)4 72 77 81 70
Fax: +33 (0)4 72 77 81 79
Opening Hours: 9h00-12h30/14h00-17h00 Monday to
Friday

### Marseille Consulate
24, avenue du Prado
13006 Marseille
Tel: +33 (0)4 91 15 72 10
Fax: +33 (0)4 91 37 47 06
Opening Hours: 9h00-12h00/14h00-17h00 Monday to
Friday

*http://www.amb-usa.fr*
American readers are advised to make note of the US
Embassy and this website address. On the day we checked
they had moved to this address from the previous website.

## American Embassies and Consulates
American Embassy
2 avenue Gabriel
75382 Paris Cedex 08
Switchboard: +33 1 43 12 22 22
Fax: +33 1 42 66 97 83

### The United States Mission to the Organization for Economic Cooperation and Development

12, avenue Raphael
75016 Paris, France
Phone: +33 1 45 24 74 11
Fax: +33 1 45 24 74 80

**The United States Mission to Unesco**
12, avenue Raphael
75016 Paris, France
Switchboard: +33 1 45 24 74 56

# Further addresses for US citizens in France

## Consulates and APP's

**Bordeaux (American Presence Post)**
10 place de la Bourse, B.P. 77,
33025 Bordeaux Cedex
Tel: 05-56-48-63-80
Fax: 05-56-51-61-97
E-mail: usabordeaux@state.gov
Website: www.amb-usa.fr/bordeaux/default.htm

**Lille (American Presence Post)**
107, rue Royale
59000 Lille
Tel: 03-28-04-25-00
Fax: 03-20-74-88-23
E-mail: usalille@state.gov
Website: www.amb-usa.fr/lille/default.htm

**Lyon (American Presence Post)**
1 Quai Jules Courmont
69002 Lyon
Tel: 04-78-38-33-03
Fax: 04-7241-7181
E-mail: *usalyon@state.gov*
Website: *www.amb-usa.fr/lyon/default.htm*

**Marseille (Consulate General)**
12, Place Varian Fry
13086 Marseille
Tel: 04-91-54-92-00
Fax: 04-91-55-09-47
Website: *www.amb-usa.fr/marseille/default.htm*

**Nice (Consular agency)**
7 avenue Gustave V, 3rd floor
06000 Nice
Tel: 04-93-88-89-55
Fax: 04-93-87-07-38
Website: *www.amb-usa.fr/marseille/nice.htm*

**Rennes (American Presence Post)**
30 quai Duguay-Trouin
35000 Rennes
Tel: 02-23-44-09-60
Fax: 02-99-35-00-92
E-mail: *usarennes@state.gov*
Website: *www.amb-usa.fr/rennes/default.htm*

**Strasbourg (Consulate General)**
15, avenue d'Alsace
67082 Strasbourg
Tel: 03-88-35-31-04
Fax: 03-88-24-06-95
Website: *www.amb-usa.fr/strasbourg/default.htm*

**Toulouse (American Presence Post)**
25, Allee Jean-Jaurès, 31000 Toulouse
Tel: 05-34-41-36-50
Fax: 05-34-41-16-19
E-mail: *usconsulate-tlse@wanadoo.fr*
Website: *www.amb-usa.fr/toulouse/default.htm*

**\* Comite National Francais de Liaison pour la Readaptation des Handicapes (CNFLRH)**

Point Handicap
38, boutevard Raspail
75007 Paris
Tel: (1)45.48.98.90
Fax: (1) 45.48.99,21
Minitel: 36,15 HANDITEL

* **Association des Paralyses**
Delegation de Paris,
17, boulevard Auguste-Blanqui,
75013 Paris
Tel: (1) 40.78.69.00
Fax: (1) 45.89.40.57

* **Union Nationale des Associations de Parents d'Enfants Inadaptes (UNAPEI)**
15, rue Coysevox
75018 Paris
Tel: (1) 42.63.84.33. (1) 42.63,08.45

* **Maison de la France**
8, avenue de l'Opera
75001 Paris
Tel: (1) 42.96.10.23
Fax: (1) 42.86.08.94

* **Centre d'Information et Documentation Jeunesse (C.I.D.J.)**
101, quai Branly
75015 Paris
Tel: (1) 44.49.12.00
Fax: (1) 40.65.02.61
Minitel: 36.15 CIDJ

* You can also consult the guide *Rousseau H Comme Handicapes*, available at Hachette Bookshops or at SCOP 4, rue Gustave-Rouanet, 75018 Paris Tel: (1) 42.52.97.00. Fax: (1) 42.52.52.50. They also have excellent advice if you are

ill, here is an extract, make sure you note the British and American hospitals, well you never know when you will need them.

...remember a drugstore (chemist) is called a 'pharmacie'. Night time and on Sundays, the Commissariat de Police of the district where you reside will inform you of the nearest drugstore (chemist) open and the address of the nearest doctor on duty. If you need to be taken to a hospital, the doctor will call an ambulance for you or you can apply to the:

**Ambulances "Assistance Publique"**
28, rue de l'Entrepot
94220 Charenton
Tel: 01.43.78.26.26
Fax: 01.45.13.65.82

**American Hospital**
63, boulevard Victor-Hugo
92202 Neuilly
Tel: 01.46.41.25.25
Fax: (1) 01.46.24.49.38
Telex: 613.344

**British Hospital Hortford**
3, rue Barbes
92300 Levallois
Tel: 01.47.58.13.12
Fax: 01.47.58.02.34

Medicine by air from home:

**Ministere des Affaires Sociales**
Service Central de la Pharmacie
14, avenue Duquesne
75007 Paris
Tel: 01.40.56.53.80. 01.40.56.60.00
Fax: 01.40.56.53.55

Open: daily except Saturdays and Sundays from 8:30 am to 12 noon and 2:00 pm to 5:30 pm. It is forbidden to import narcotics into France unless you obtain beforehand a special authorization from the French narcotic office at the address mentioned above.

# French Canada

Europeans often forget the exciting and vibrant use of French in Canada. Here we present some useful Canadian contacts.

*http://www.britainincanada.org/* This is the British Embassy in Ottawa.

*Mailing address*
**British High Commission**
80 Elgin Street
Ottawa
Ontario K1P 5K7

**Contacts**

*Main*
Office hours: 8:30am – 4:30pm
Switchboard: 8:30am – 5:00pm
Tel: 1 613 237 1530
Fax: 1 613 237 7980

*Passports*
Office hours: 9:00am – 12.00 noon
Switchboard: 10:00am – 3:00pm
Tel: 1 613 237 1303
FaxL 1 613 237 6537
**Visa/Immigration**
Office hours: by e-appointment only
Switchboard: 10:00am – 1:00pm
Tel: 1 613 237 2008
Fax: 1 613 232 2533

**The British Council**
1000 De La Gauchetière Street West
Suite 4200
Montreal, Quebec   H3B 4W5
Tel.: 1 514 866 5863 (extensions 2222 and 2223)
Fax: 1 514 866 5322
Email: *education.enquiries@ca.britishcouncil.org*

**British Consulate General and British Trade & Investment Office**
777 Bay Street
Suite 2800
Toronto
Ontario   M5G 2G2
Tel: 416 593 1290
Fax: 416 593 1229
Email: *toronto@britainincanada.org*
Trade & Investment website: *http://www.uktradeinvest canada.org*

**British Canadian Chamber of Trade & Commerce**
PO Box 1358, Station 'K'
Toronto
Ontario M4P 3J4
Tel: 1 416 502 0847
Fax: 1 416 502 9319
Email: *central@bcctc.ca*
Website: *http://www.bcctc.ca*

**VisitBritain**
5915 Airport Rd
Suite 120
Mississauga
Ontario L4V 1T1
Office hours: 09:00-17:00
Switchboard: 10:00-18:00
Tel: 1 888 Visit UK (847 4885)
Fax: 1 905 405 1835

Email: *britinfo@visitbritain.org*
Website: *http://www.visitbritain.com/ca*

## Vancouver
**British Consulate General**
1111 Melville Street
Suite 800
Vancouver
British Columbia V6E 3V6
Tel:  604 683 4421
Fax: 604 681 0693
Email: *vancouver@britainincanada.org*
More ... see *Contact us*

PO Box 2930
Vancouver
British Columbia V6B 3X4
Tel: 1 604 222 1920
Fax: 1 604 222 1956
Website: *http://www.bcctc.ca*

## Calgary
**British Trade Office**
250 6th Avenue SW
Suite 1500
Calgary
Alberta  TP2 3H7
Tel: 403 705 1755
Fax: 403 538 0121
Email: *calgary@britainincanada.org*
More ... see *Contact us*

# US Consulate

Here is what they say.

## US Consular Services

*The Consular Section of the U.S. Embassy is located at 490 Sussex Drive in Ottawa, Ontario. The Embassy and Consular Section's mailing address is:*
P.O. Box 866, Station B
Ottawa,
Ontario K1P 5T1
Tel: 613.238.5335
Fax: 613.688.3082

**Office de la langue française:** *http://www.oqlf.gouv.qc.ca*
Office de la langue française
25 West Sherbrooke Street
Montreal, Quebec
H2X 1X4
Tel: (514) 873-8277
Fax: (514) 873-3488

**Office of the Commissioner of Official Languages:** *http://www.ocol-clo.gc.ca*

**Office of the Commissioner of Official Languages**
344 Slater Street, 3rd Floor
Ottawa,
Ontario K1A 0T8
Tel: (613) 995-0648
Fax: (613) 943-2255

**Treasury Board Secretariat – Official Languages Branch:** *http://www.hrma-agrh.gc.ca/ollo/index_e.asp*

**Canadian Translators and Interpreters Council:** *http://www.cttic.org/*

All of the above are on *http://www.canadianheritage.gc.ca/guide/liens_adresses_e.html*

Their contact details are:

**Official Languages Support Programs Branch**
Canadian Heritage
15 Eddy Street, 7th floor
Gatineau,
Quebec K1A 0M5

# Useful Canadian sites

http://www.trailcanada.com/travel/french-travel-phrases.asp
This gives useful advice over the differences between French
spoken in France and French spoken in Canada.

http://www.lambic.co.uk/canada/
Just in case you get the 'bug' and want to move to Canada,
have a look and see what this tells you.

http://www.emploietudiant.qc.ca/en/liens.html
Some great links here, all of which are relevant to Canada.
This is a site that helps students enter the job market in
Canada. Their contact details are on the site.

*http://www.stcum.qc.ca/metro/*
Details about the Montreal Metro

*http://www.viarail.ca/fr_index.html*
Canadian Rail

*http://www.postescanada.ca/splash.asp*
Candian Postal service

# Index of English Words

# Index of French Words

Toutes mes félicitations au
papa et à la maman pour cet
heureux évènement.

J'espère vous revoir
bientôt et faire la connaissance
d'Eva à Londres.